MASSACHUSETTS TEST PREP
English Language Arts
Reading Workbook
Grade 6

© 2016 by Test Master Press Massachusetts

All rights reserved. No part of this book may be reproduced or transmitted in any form or by any means, electronic, mechanical, photocopying, recording, or otherwise without prior written permission.

ISBN 978-1540570000

English Language Arts, Reading Workbook, Grade 6

CONTENTS

Introduction   4

Reading Comprehension Exercises
Set 1 – Literary Texts   5
Set 2 – Informational Texts   15
Set 3 – Literary and Informational Texts   25
Set 4 – Literary and Informational Texts   35
Set 5 – Paired Literary Texts   45
Set 6 – Paired Informational Texts   51
Set 7 – Literary Texts   57
Set 8 – Informational Texts   67
Set 9 – Literary and Informational Texts   77
Set 10 – Literary and Informational Texts   87
Set 11 – Paired Literary Texts   97
Set 12 – Paired Informational Texts   103

Answer Key   **109**
Set 1 – Literary Texts   110
Set 2 – Informational Texts   112
Set 3 – Literary and Informational Texts   114
Set 4 – Literary and Informational Texts   116
Set 5 – Paired Literary Texts   118
Set 6 – Paired Informational Texts   119
Set 7 – Literary Texts   120
Set 8 – Informational Texts   122
Set 9 – Literary and Informational Texts   124
Set 10 – Literary and Informational Texts   126
Set 11 – Paired Literary Texts   128
Set 12 – Paired Informational Texts   129

English Language Arts, Reading Workbook, Grade 6

INTRODUCTION
For Parents, Teachers, and Tutors

About the Book

This workbook will develop the reading skills that students are expected to have, while preparing students for the MCAS tests. The focus of the book is on developing reading comprehension skills, but the complementary writing and language skills are also covered.

Massachusetts Curriculum Frameworks

In 2017, new *Massachusetts Curriculum Frameworks* were introduced. Beginning in spring 2018, the MCAS tests will assess the 2017 *Massachusetts Curriculum Frameworks*. All the exercises and questions in this book cover the skills listed in the 2017 *Massachusetts Curriculum Frameworks*.

Ongoing Reading Comprehension Practice

The aim of this book is to give students ongoing reading comprehension practice without the stress of long passages and question sets. Each set contains four short texts with questions, or two texts in paired sets. By completing each set, students will gain experience with a range of passage types, become familiar with common question types, practice understanding and responding to texts, develop confidence, and master all the reading skills needed.

Developing Reading Skills

The *Massachusetts Curriculum Frameworks* describe what students are expected to know. The reading standards are divided into two areas: Reading Standards for Literature and Reading Standards for Informational Text. This workbook includes sets that focus only on literature, only on informational texts, and mixed sets that cover both. This book also includes paired passages, where students synthesize and integrate information from two texts.

Introducing Core Skills

Each passage in this workbook includes a Core Skills Practice exercise that focuses on one key reading, writing, or language skill. These exercises will introduce students to the key skills and help students transition to the more challenging ELA standards.

Preparing for the MCAS Tests

Students in Massachusetts are assessed each year by taking the MCAS tests. This workbook will prepare students for these assessments. The reading comprehension skills developed are those that will be assessed, so the strong skills gained will help students perform well. The workbook also provides experience understanding, analyzing, and responding to passages, as well as practice answering multiple choice, short response, and essay questions.

Reading Comprehension

Set 1

Literary Texts

Instructions

Read each passage. Complete the exercise under each passage.

Then complete the questions following each passage. For each multiple-choice question, fill in the circle for the correct answer. For other types of questions, follow the instructions given. Some of the questions require a written answer. Write your answer on the lines provided.

Snowed In

"HQ, this is Nord, do you copy?" Dr. Nord spoke into the microphone. He tapped away at various buttons and waited a few moments.

"Guess I'm stuck here for another day," Nord said as he hung his head.

Two days ago, a snow storm had hit the research bunker he was working in. The howling winds had battered against the walls of the bunker for hours, while snow had piled up and threatened to cover the bunker completely. Dr. Nord had stayed safely inside the research bunker. No matter how deafening the wind became or how hard the snow seemed to slam into the bunker, Dr. Nord remained calm. He knew that the bunker could withstand anything that the harsh weather could throw at it.

While the bunker stayed perfectly fine, the communications tower had been lost. Dr. Nord wasn't worried though. He knew someone would come looking for him.

CORE SKILLS PRACTICE

Many stories involve cause and effect. The cause is the reason for something. The effect is what happens. Answer the question below about cause and effect.

What effect does the storm have on Dr. Nord?

_____

_____

_____

_____

_____

1   In the second paragraph, the phrase "hung his head" shows that Nord is –

   Ⓐ   frightened

   Ⓑ   disappointed

   Ⓒ   freezing

   Ⓓ   famished

2   How does Nord feel about having lost all communication?

   Ⓐ   Puzzled

   Ⓑ   Delighted

   Ⓒ   Calm

   Ⓓ   Lonesome

3   What is the most likely setting of the passage?

   Ⓐ   The Arctic

   Ⓑ   The Sahara Desert

   Ⓒ   The Amazon rainforest

   Ⓓ   The Florida wetlands

4   In the first sentence, Nord says "Do you copy?" What does this phrase help readers understand?

   Ⓐ   He is speaking on the radio.

   Ⓑ   He is a scientist.

   Ⓒ   He is stuck somewhere alone.

   Ⓓ   He is writing a report.

The Miner

After days and days of failure, the tough old miner picked up a lump of gold from the ground. After so many disappointments, he could barely bring himself to imagine it could really be gold. He reminded himself that he had found it before, and he could find it again. After staring at it for a few moments, he bit it sharply between his teeth.

"She sure is gold!" he proclaimed excitedly, before picking up his pickaxe.

The miner wandered around in front of the rock wall for a few minutes, before swinging his heavy pickaxe into it. After a few hours of mining, the miner had a small bowl full of gleaming golden nuggets. He set off happily for home, whistling all the way there.

CORE SKILLS PRACTICE

Imagine how the story would be different if it was written from the miner's point of view. The story could reveal more of the miner's thoughts and feelings. Write a paragraph from the miner's point of view describing his search for gold.

_____

_____

_____

_____

_____

_____

_____

1. The second paragraph states that the miner "proclaimed excitedly." Which word means about the same as <u>proclaimed</u>?
   - Ⓐ Declared
   - Ⓑ Argued
   - Ⓒ Whispered
   - Ⓓ Assumed

2. Why did the miner most likely bite the gold?
   - Ⓐ He was confused.
   - Ⓑ He needed to check that it was gold.
   - Ⓒ He was hungry.
   - Ⓓ He wanted to see how much it was worth.

3. Which set of words from the passage is an example of alliteration?
   - Ⓐ *lump of gold*
   - Ⓑ *bit it sharply*
   - Ⓒ *gleaming golden nuggets*
   - Ⓓ *whistling a happy tune*

4. The first paragraph of the passage shows that the miner feels –
   - Ⓐ embarrassed
   - Ⓑ puzzled
   - Ⓒ impatient
   - Ⓓ discouraged

What Caterpillars Do

What, oh what do caterpillars do?
They don't do much but chew and chew.
What, oh what do caterpillars know?
They don't know much but how to grow.

They can't watch TV, go fishing, or cry,
But they can turn into a butterfly.
That is more than I can do,
No matter how much I chew, chew, chew.

CORE SKILLS PRACTICE

What do you think is the main theme of the poem? How does the poet communicate the theme?

_____

_____

_____

_____

_____

_____

1. Which word best describes the mood of the speaker?
   - Ⓐ Gloomy
   - Ⓑ Mysterious
   - Ⓒ Frustrating
   - **Ⓓ Cheerful**

2. Which literary device is used in the poem?
   - Ⓐ Flashback
   - **Ⓑ Repetition**
   - Ⓒ Similes
   - Ⓓ Personification

3. What is the rhyme pattern of each stanza of the poem?
   - Ⓐ Every line rhymes.
   - Ⓑ The second and fourth lines rhyme.
   - Ⓒ The first and last lines rhyme.
   - **Ⓓ There are two sets of rhyming lines.**

4. In the poem, what does turning into a butterfly represent?
   - Ⓐ A goal the poet wishes that she could achieve
   - Ⓑ A change that the poet has to accept
   - **Ⓒ Something special that only a caterpillar can do**
   - Ⓓ A way the caterpillar entertains itself

Flying High

My family and I live near the airport. Some people think that's a bad thing, but I think it's great. I've always loved watching the airplanes fly way up high. They soar overhead like giant metallic birds. They seem huge as they pass overhead, and it amazes me that something so massive is able to fly. Sometimes I think about who is on the plane and where they are going. The planes might be mainly full of people traveling for work, but I like to imagine they are full of people on their way to explore exciting new lands.

My mom and dad always complain about the noise, especially late at night. But not me! I can hear the planes as I fall asleep, but that just makes me dream that I'm on my way to some exciting location. When I grow up and move into my own place, I hope it's near an airport too. Maybe I'll even fly an airplane one day. That would be a dream come true.

CORE SKILLS PRACTICE

The narrator and his parents have different views on whether it is a good thing to live near an airport. How do you think you would feel about living near an airport? Use details from the passage to support your answer.

_____

_____

_____

_____

_____

English Language Arts, Reading Workbook, Grade 6

1. Which two words from the passage have about the same meaning?
   - Ⓐ *airplanes, airport*
   - Ⓑ *bad, great*
   - Ⓒ *fly, soar*
   - Ⓓ *noise, dream*

2. How is the narrator similar to his parents?
   - Ⓐ He likes watching the airplanes.
   - Ⓑ He finds the sound of the airplanes annoying.
   - Ⓒ He wants to fly an airplane some day.
   - Ⓓ He lives near the airport.

3. When do the narrator's parents find the planes most annoying?
   - Ⓐ Early in the morning
   - Ⓑ In the afternoon
   - Ⓒ Around dinner time
   - Ⓓ Late at night

4. Based on the passage, which of these is NOT a quality of the narrator?
   - Ⓐ Imaginative
   - Ⓑ Positive
   - Ⓒ Adventurous
   - Ⓓ Bad-tempered

5 Identify the simile in the passage and explain why the author used it. Use information from the passage to support your answer.

Reading Comprehension

Set 2

Informational Texts

Instructions

Read each passage. Complete the exercise under each passage.

Then complete the questions following each passage. For each multiple-choice question, fill in the circle for the correct answer. For other types of questions, follow the instructions given. Some of the questions require a written answer. Write your answer on the lines provided.

Brain in a Bottle

Did you know that the remains of Einstein's brain are stored at Princeton Hospital in New Jersey? Dr. Thomas Harvey was the doctor who had to conduct the initial autopsy on Einstein in 1955. Harvey removed Einstein's brain without permission from Einstein's family. He carefully sliced it into sections to keep for research. It was an unethical thing to do, but it has provided valuable information to scientists. It remains controversial to this day. There are some who argue that it should never have been done. There are others who believe that the information that could potentially be gained was worth it.

There are now at least three published papers relating to the study of Einstein's brain. Scientists have attempted to understand what made Einstein a genius, and have determined that his brain did have some unique features. One part of the brain called the parietal lobe was larger than normal. It was also not separated into two compartments, as it is in normal brains. It is thought that this might explain Einstein's intelligence, creativity, and mathematical ability.

CORE SKILLS PRACTICE

Scientists contrasted Einstein's brain with those of other people. Describe **two** differences that scientists found.

1. _____

_____

2. _____

_____

1. Which meaning of the word conduct is used in the first paragraph?
   - Ⓐ To transmit heat energy
   - Ⓑ To behave in a certain way
   - Ⓒ To lead a vocal group
   - Ⓓ To carry out

2. Why does the author begin the passage with a question?
   - Ⓐ To get readers interested in the topic of the passage
   - Ⓑ To show that Dr. Thomas Harvey did the wrong thing
   - Ⓒ To suggest that readers should research the topic
   - Ⓓ To explain how scientists learn by asking questions

3. What is the passage mainly about?
   - Ⓐ How Einstein's brain was kept
   - Ⓑ How scientists conduct research
   - Ⓒ Why doctors should follow rules
   - Ⓓ Why Einstein was a genius

4. Which sentence best summarizes both the negative and positive aspects of what Harvey did?
   - Ⓐ *Harvey removed Einstein's brain without permission from Einstein's family.*
   - Ⓑ *It was an unethical thing to do, but it has provided valuable information to scientists.*
   - Ⓒ *It remains controversial to this day.*
   - Ⓓ *There are now at least three published papers relating to the study of Einstein's brain.*

Hillary Clinton

Hillary Clinton was born on October 26, 1947. She was the First Lady of the United States from 1993 to 2001, as the wife of President Bill Clinton. In 2001, she became a senator for the state of New York. She remained in this role until 2009. In January of 2009, she became the 67th United States Secretary of State, serving under President Barack Obama. Just prior to this, Clinton was also considered as a candidate to run for president. She remained as Secretary of State until February, 2013.

CORE SKILLS PRACTICE

In 2014, Hillary Clinton published a memoir titled *Hard Choices*. The book focused on her time as Secretary of State. Describe how a memoir would be different from the passage above.

_____

_____

_____

_____

_____

_____

_____

_____

1. Which meaning of the word serving is used in the passage?
   - Ⓐ Providing customers with goods
   - Ⓑ Being in the armed services
   - Ⓒ Giving people food or drink
   - Ⓓ Working for somebody

2. Where would this passage most likely be found?
   - Ⓐ In an encyclopedia
   - Ⓑ In a travel guide
   - Ⓒ In a newspaper
   - Ⓓ In a book of short stories

3. Place Hillary Clinton's roles in politics in order from first to last. Write the numbers 1, 2, 3, and 4 on the lines to show your choices.

   ____ Senator for New York

   ____ First Lady

   ____ Secretary of State

   ____ Candidate for president

4. Which of these would make the best opening sentence for a summary of the passage?
   - Ⓐ Hillary Clinton has had a successful and varied career in politics.
   - Ⓑ Hillary Clinton met Bill Clinton while studying at Yale Law School.
   - Ⓒ While First Lady, Hillary Clinton played an active political role.
   - Ⓓ In 2008, some considered that Hillary Clinton could become America's first female president.

Antique Map

It's really easy and fun to make a map look like it's an old antique. You'll need to print out a map or get permission to use an old map that is no longer needed. You'll also need to make some strong black tea (make sure you let it cool down) and a spray bottle to put the tea in.

Step 1: Place the map on a clean flat surface that will be easy to clean afterwards.

Step 2: Soak the entire map by spraying it evenly with black tea.

Step 3: Gently lift the map after it is sprayed to make sure it does not stick to the flat surface.

Step 4: Allow the map to dry and repeat steps 1 to 3 until you achieve the desired effect.

Step 5: Add some marks and tears to the edges of map.

CORE SKILLS PRACTICE

Describe **two** features of the map that make it appear older than it really is.

1. _____

_____

2. _____

_____

1. What is the main purpose of the first sentence of the passage?
   - Ⓐ To show the items needed for the project
   - Ⓑ To explain what makes maps look older
   - Ⓒ To encourage people to want to complete the project
   - Ⓓ To show that the author has experience with the project

2. In which step is the black tea first needed?
   - Ⓐ Step 1
   - Ⓑ Step 2
   - Ⓒ Step 3
   - Ⓓ Step 4

3. What is the most likely reason it is important to let the black tea cool down?
   - Ⓐ So the map does not get ruined
   - Ⓑ So the map changes color
   - Ⓒ So the tea cannot be consumed
   - Ⓓ So the tea does not burn anyone

4. In step 2, what does the word soak suggest?
   - Ⓐ That the map will quickly change color
   - Ⓑ That the map should have a light covering of tea
   - Ⓒ That a lot of tea should be used
   - Ⓓ That there should be more tea at the edges of the map

Defeat at Waterloo

Napoleon Bonaparte was a legendary military leader during the late stages of the French Revolution. He was leader of the French Army and led the French to wins in many major battles. He later became Emperor of France and continued to lead the French through many successful battles. For over ten years, the French seemed unbeatable.

The French Army was finally defeated in 1815 at the Battle of Waterloo. The French Army was again led by Napoleon, but this time he was on the losing side. An enormous coalition of European forces battled against the French and won.

The events of Napoleon's life fired the imagination of great writers and filmmakers. Their works have continued to foster the legend of Napoleon.

This 1801 painting by Jacques-Louis David is titled *Napoleon at the Saint-Bernard Pass*. It shows Napoleon as a brave and capable leader.

CORE SKILLS PRACTICE

What can you infer about why Napoleon's French Army was finally defeated? Explain your answer.

_____

_____

_____

_____

1 What does the word <u>fired</u> suggest about the writers and filmmakers?

> **The events of Napoleon's life fired the imagination of great writers and filmmakers.**

- Ⓐ They were angered by Napoleon.
- Ⓑ They were paid well for their work.
- Ⓒ They were forced to write about Napoleon.
- Ⓓ They were inspired by Napoleon.

2 Which word would the author most likely use to describe Napoleon as a military leader?

- Ⓐ Imaginative
- Ⓑ Impressive
- Ⓒ Stubborn
- Ⓓ Average

3 What is the second paragraph mainly about?

- Ⓐ Napoleon's success as a leader
- Ⓑ Napoleon's eventual downfall
- Ⓒ The importance of Napoleon to France
- Ⓓ How Napoleon is remembered today

4 The painting included in the passage is mainly used to show –

- Ⓐ how Napoleon is remembered
- Ⓑ what caused Napoleon's downfall
- Ⓒ the strategies Napoleon used in battle
- Ⓓ how enemies of France feared Napoleon

5   Was Napoleon Bonaparte a successful military leader? Use information from the passage to support your answer.

Reading Comprehension

Set 3

Literary and Informational Texts

Instructions

Read each passage. Complete the exercise under each passage.

Then complete the questions following each passage. For each multiple-choice question, fill in the circle for the correct answer. For other types of questions, follow the instructions given. Some of the questions require a written answer. Write your answer on the lines provided.

Belarus

Belarus is a landlocked country in Eastern Europe. It has a population of around 9.5 million. The capital of Belarus is Minsk. Minsk has an estimated population of just over two million. Around forty percent of the country is forested. This makes agriculture one of Belarus' important industries. The other major industry is manufacturing, with Belarus known for making tractors, trucks, and other large equipment. Following the collapse of the Soviet Union, Belarus declared its independence in 1991. Belarus has two official languages: Belarusian and Russian. Belarus continues to have close ties with Russia. Almost half of all the goods produced and exported are sold to Russia, and it also imports many of the goods it needs from Russia.

CORE SKILLS PRACTICE

While Belarus is no longer part of Russia, it still has connections to Russia. Describe **two** ways Belarus is still connected to Russia today.

1. _____

_____

2. _____

_____

1   Which sentence from the passage is supported by the map?
    Ⓐ   *Belarus is a landlocked country in Eastern Europe.*
    Ⓑ   *Minsk has an estimated population of just over two million.*
    Ⓒ   *Around forty percent of the country is forested.*
    Ⓓ   *Belarus has two official languages: Belarusian and Russian.*

2   Which of the following would NOT be found in Belarus?
    Ⓐ   Forest
    Ⓑ   Ocean
    Ⓒ   River
    Ⓓ   Lake

3   Where would this passage most likely be found?
    Ⓐ   In a science magazine
    Ⓑ   In a book of short stories
    Ⓒ   In an encyclopedia
    Ⓓ   In a travel guide

4   What does the word <u>landlocked</u> show about Belarus?
    Ⓐ   It is surrounded by land on all sides.
    Ⓑ   It is made up mainly of forests.
    Ⓒ   It was once part of a larger nation.
    Ⓓ   It has been affected by civil wars.

Magnetic North

The compass was invented in ancient China around 247 B.C. It became popular for use in navigation by the 11th century. In those early days, they were an essential tool for sailors and explorers. Militaries also relied on them for land navigation, or orienteering. Today, compasses are still used by some sailors, but are not as important as they once were. New technologies have replaced the compass in many ways. Sailors now often use computerized systems and GPS to navigate. Computerized compasses will tell you the direction faster and more accurately than an actual compass. Many cell phones even have built-in compasses. Even with these technologies, learning to use a compass is a useful skill. They are often used by people doing activities like hiking or orienteering.

Most compass devices consist of a dial with north, east, south, and west marked on them. The compass has a spinning needle mounted in the middle. The needle is magnetized and aligns itself with the Earth's magnetic field. This results in the compass needle always facing toward the north.

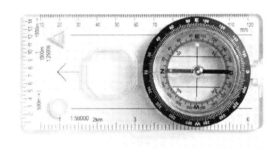

Modern compasses are small, light-weight, and easy to use.

CORE SKILLS PRACTICE

Why are compasses less important to sailors today than they once were? Explain your answer.

_____

_____

_____

_____

1 According to the passage, what original use of compasses is still a common use today?

- Ⓐ Sailing
- Ⓑ Exploring
- Ⓒ Hiking
- Ⓓ Orienteering

2 What does the photograph best show?

- Ⓐ How to use a compass
- Ⓑ What a compass looks like
- Ⓒ What a compass can be used for
- Ⓓ When the compass was invented

3 What is the second paragraph mainly about?

- Ⓐ How a compass works
- Ⓑ How compasses have changed
- Ⓒ Common uses of a compass
- Ⓓ The invention of the compass

4 The word <u>navigate</u> is based on the Latin root *navis*, which means –

- Ⓐ ship
- Ⓑ time
- Ⓒ land
- Ⓓ new

Hide and Seek

Jeremy pulled the door to his closet shut slowly. "Ready or not, here I come!" Vanessa yelled from the kitchen.

Jeremy snickered a little. He knew Vanessa would never find him in his closet. He decided he would wait quietly in the closet until he heard Vanessa enter his room. Then he would leap out of the closet and scare her. He thought the game was childish, but Vanessa had begged him to play. He had finally given in, but now he planned to pay her back.

Vanessa could be heard ruffling through different places for a short while before everything went quiet. Jeremy listened closely, but he couldn't hear a sound. He leaned over and peeked out the door.

"Ahhhhh!" Jeremy let out a yell like he had just seen a ghost.

Vanessa's face was right in front of the closet door staring back at him.

"Found you," Vanessa giggled and ran off.

CORE SKILLS PRACTICE

Irony occurs when something happens that is very different from what is expected to happen. Describe the irony in the passage.

_____

_____

_____

_____

_____

English Language Arts, Reading Workbook, Grade 6

1. Which word means about the same as <u>snickered</u>?
   - Ⓐ Laughed
   - Ⓑ Sighed
   - Ⓒ Chatted
   - Ⓓ Coughed

2. Which sentence from the passage contains a simile?
   - Ⓐ *Jeremy pulled the door to his closet shut slowly.*
   - Ⓑ *He knew Vanessa would never find him in his closet.*
   - Ⓒ *Jeremy leaned over and peeked out the door.*
   - Ⓓ *Jeremy let out a yell like he had just seen a ghost.*

3. Why does Jeremy most likely close the closet door slowly?
   - Ⓐ So he does not get stuck in the closet
   - Ⓑ So he can still see out of the closet
   - Ⓒ So Vanessa does not hear him
   - Ⓓ So he does not scare Vanessa

4. Based on the passage, Vanessa is most likely Jeremy's —
   - Ⓐ older sister
   - Ⓑ younger sister
   - Ⓒ mother
   - Ⓓ aunt

Danny's Homework

Danny was sitting down on the rug and tapping away at the keys on his laptop. He was working on his homework, when all of a sudden his laptop turned off.

"No!" he panicked, pressing the power button repeatedly. He stood up and ran over to his desk with his laptop. Plugging it into the charger, he waited as the laptop booted up again.

"Ding!" said the laptop excitedly as it started up. Danny let out a huge sigh when he saw that his homework file had automatically saved.

"That was a close call," he sighed.

CORE SKILLS PRACTICE

How does the author show how worried Danny was about losing his work?

_____

_____

_____

_____

_____

_____

1. Read this sentence from the passage.

   "Ding!" said the laptop excitedly as it started up.

   Which literary device does the author use in this sentence?
   - Ⓐ Simile
   - Ⓑ Alliteration
   - Ⓒ Imagery
   - Ⓓ Personification

2. Why did the laptop most likely shut down?
   - Ⓐ It had a fault.
   - Ⓑ It ran out of power.
   - Ⓒ Danny knocked it over.
   - Ⓓ Danny shut the lid.

3. Which word best describes how Danny feels when he sees that his homework has saved?
   - Ⓐ Relieved
   - Ⓑ Alarmed
   - Ⓒ Stressed
   - Ⓓ Excited

4. In the last sentence, what does "a close call" refer to?
   - Ⓐ A near miss
   - Ⓑ An exciting event
   - Ⓒ A foolish action
   - Ⓓ A serious problem

5 What would Danny be most likely to do the next time he uses his laptop to do his homework? Use details from the passage to support your answer.

Reading Comprehension

Set 4

Literary and Informational Texts

Instructions

Read each passage. Complete the exercise under each passage.

Then complete the questions following each passage. For each multiple-choice question, fill in the circle for the correct answer. For other types of questions, follow the instructions given. Some of the questions require a written answer. Write your answer on the lines provided.

Ruler of Macedon

Alexander the Great is one of the most noteworthy kings of all time. He was king of Macedon in north-eastern Greece in 336 B.C. By the age of 30, Alexander the Great had created one of the largest empires in ancient history. He was responsible for the fall of the Persian king Darius III, among many other grand accomplishments. The tactical achievements of Alexander are still taught throughout the world in military academies today.

This 1895 painting depicts Alexander the Great being tutored by Aristotle.

CORE SKILLS PRACTICE

The author includes details to support the idea that Alexander the Great was a noteworthy king. Identify **two** supporting details from the passage.

1. _____

_____

2. _____

_____

1. Which word means about the same as <u>noteworthy</u>?
   - Ⓐ Enduring
   - Ⓑ Celebrated
   - Ⓒ Significant
   - Ⓓ Damaging

2. Which detail best shows that Alexander the Great is still appreciated today?
   - Ⓐ He was king of Macedon.
   - Ⓑ He created one of the largest empires ever.
   - Ⓒ He caused the fall of the Persian king Darius III.
   - Ⓓ His achievements are taught in military academies.

3. What type of passage is "Ruler of Macedon"?
   - Ⓐ Realistic fiction
   - Ⓑ Biography
   - Ⓒ Historical fiction
   - Ⓓ Autobiography

4. The word <u>tactical</u> contains the base word <u>tactic</u>. <u>Tactic</u> means –
   - Ⓐ problem
   - Ⓑ method
   - Ⓒ thoughts
   - Ⓓ solution

Bananas

April 14

Dear Aunt Janine,

Today Dad told me that I've been opening a banana wrong all of my life. I thought he was messing with me!

Then Dad looked up some videos on the Internet and showed me how a monkey opens a banana. They don't do it from the stem end. They grab the tip, pinch it, and peel one side down, and then peel the other side. It's so easy. I have to admit I was impressed.

Well, now I know I've been opening a banana wrong all of my life. I don't know what is worse – having to admit that Dad was right or having to admit that a monkey is smarter than me!

Bye for now,

Jacky

CORE SKILLS PRACTICE

How can you tell that Jacky will probably change how she eats bananas?

_____

_____

_____

_____

_____

1. What does the sentence below mean?

   I thought he was messing with me!

   - Ⓐ I thought he was wrong.
   - Ⓑ I thought he was teasing me.
   - Ⓒ I thought he was cleaning.
   - Ⓓ I thought he was mad at me.

2. What does a monkey do first when peeling a banana?
   - Ⓐ Pinches the tip of the banana
   - Ⓑ Grabs the tip of the banana
   - Ⓒ Peels one side of the banana down
   - Ⓓ Squeezes the stem of the banana

3. How does Jacky most likely feel when she sees how monkeys eat bananas?
   - Ⓐ Annoyed
   - Ⓑ Puzzled
   - Ⓒ Surprised
   - Ⓓ Unimpressed

4. In which sentence does <u>tip</u> mean the same as in the passage?
   - Ⓐ The coach gave me a good <u>tip</u> for how to make three-point shots.
   - Ⓑ I sharpened the pencil until the <u>tip</u> was nice and sharp.
   - Ⓒ Morgan asked me to help him <u>tip</u> the bark into the garden.
   - Ⓓ It's important to remember to <u>tip</u> when you get good service.

The Human Skeleton

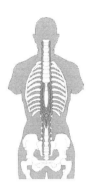

Did you know that there are over 206 bones in the adult human skeleton? Newborn babies have over 270 bones. As a newborn baby grows, some of their bones are fused together.

The skeleton performs several very important functions within our body. These include providing a support framework, protecting vital organs, and playing a crucial role in the generation of blood cells. Bones are also a storage site for many of the minerals our bodies need.

Osteoporosis is a medical condition that occurs when the bones become less dense. This makes them weak and brittle, and can lead to bones fracturing easily. When a bone is very brittle, something as simple as coughing can result in a fracture. Osteoporosis can affect anyone, but is most common in women. Luckily, preventing osteoporosis is quite simple. A diet high in calcium and sufficient exercise will usually prevent osteoporosis.

CORE SKILLS PRACTICE

You can often work out what a word means by how it is used in a passage. Locate the words below in the passage. Write a definition of each word.

fused: _____

brittle: _____

fracture: _____

sufficient: _____

English Language Arts, Reading Workbook, Grade 6

1. Which two words from the passage have about the same meaning?
   - Ⓐ *storage, minerals*
   - Ⓑ *weak, dense*
   - Ⓒ *adult, newborn*
   - Ⓓ *vital, crucial*

2. Complete the web below using information from the passage.

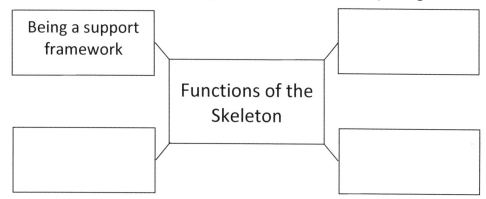

3. According to the passage, how are adults different from children?
   - Ⓐ They have more bones.
   - Ⓑ They have fewer bones.
   - Ⓒ Their bones have more purposes.
   - Ⓓ Their bones have fewer purposes.

4. Which sentence from the passage gives a cause and effect?
   - Ⓐ *Newborn babies have over 270 bones.*
   - Ⓑ *The skeleton performs several very important functions within our body.*
   - Ⓒ *When a bone is very brittle, something as simple as coughing can result in a fracture.*
   - Ⓓ *Osteoporosis can affect anyone, but is most common in women.*

The Desert Oasis

Serian had walked for days in the desert. He was from a village near the desert and he had been raised to know of its dangers. He knew he must not let it defeat him. No matter how tired he felt, he could not allow himself to sit down and rest. He must keep walking over one dune and then another until he found the land beyond.

He scuffled across the hot desert sand, waiting for nightfall to ease the sweltering heat. Serian reached the peak of a sand dune. As he stared off into the distance, he noticed something glimmering. He shielded his eyes from the harsh light and tried to focus his eyes. Off in the distance, he saw an oasis filled with plants. Serian closed his eyes and shook his head back and forth, as if testing to see if the image would shake loose. When he opened his eyes, the oasis was still there. He smiled for the first time in days as he powered on toward the oasis. He could now rest, take on water, and continue on his way.

CORE SKILLS PRACTICE

In what way is Serian's journey like a quest? Explain.

_____

_____

_____

_____

_____

1   Serian's journey through the desert has a lesson about –
    Ⓐ   planning
    Ⓑ   determination
    Ⓒ   wisdom
    Ⓓ   patience

2   The phrase "powered on" at the end of the passage shows that Serian –
    Ⓐ   wandered slowly
    Ⓑ   walked with enthusiasm
    Ⓒ   needed more energy
    Ⓓ   was overheating

3   Why is Serian keen for nightfall to come?
    Ⓐ   So he can finally rest
    Ⓑ   Because it will be cooler
    Ⓒ   Because he might be able to spot lights
    Ⓓ   So he can use the stars to guide him

4   What does the photograph in the passage mainly show?
    Ⓐ   Why Serian is seeking out the land beyond
    Ⓑ   How important it is that Serian does not stop
    Ⓒ   How vast and empty the desert is
    Ⓓ   Why Serian is unsure if the oasis is real

5 How do you think Serian feels when he sees the oasis? Use information from the passage to support your answer.

Reading Comprehension

Set 5

Paired Literary Texts

Instructions

This set contains a pair of passages. Read each passage on its own first. Complete the exercise under each passage. Then complete the questions following each passage.

For each multiple-choice question, fill in the circle for the correct answer. For other types of questions, follow the instructions given. Some of the questions require a written answer. Write your answer on the lines provided.

After reading both passages, you will answer one or more additional questions. You will use information from both passages to answer these questions. Write your answers on the lines provided.

The Dog and the River

A dog was crossing a river by walking across a log. He had a small but juicy piece of meat in his mouth. He walked slowly across the log, while being careful not to lose his balance. As he looked down, he saw his own reflection in the water. He mistook the reflection for another dog. As he stared at the dog, he realized that the piece of meat it was carrying was larger than his own. He immediately dropped his own piece of meat and attacked the other dog to get the larger piece.

As he barked at the dog, his piece of meat fell from his mouth and into the water below. His paw struck at his reflection, only to hit the water below. At that moment, he realized that the other dog was only his reflection. He stared sadly at his small piece of meat as it floated away.

CORE SKILLS PRACTICE

How can you tell that the events in the passage could not really happen?

_____

_____

_____

_____

_____

_____

_____

1. What type of passage is "The Dog and the River"?
   - Ⓐ Tall tale
   - Ⓑ Mystery
   - Ⓒ Science fiction
   - Ⓓ Fable

2. What is the main lesson the dog learns in the passage?
   - Ⓐ Bigger is usually better.
   - Ⓑ Be thankful for what you have.
   - Ⓒ Be careful when crossing rivers.
   - Ⓓ Fighting does not achieve anything.

3. Which of the following is the best summary of the passage?
   - Ⓐ A dog with a small piece of meat thinks his reflection is a dog with a large piece of meat. He tries to get the large piece and ends up with no meat.
   - Ⓑ A dog sees another dog with a better piece of meat. He drops his own piece. He loses the fight with the other dog.
   - Ⓒ A dog thinks he sees a dog with a larger piece of meat. He drops his own meat. Then he realizes that the other piece of meat is not real. He regrets the decision that he made.
   - Ⓓ A dog is crossing a river with a small piece of meat. He drops the meat into the river. He is unable to get it back.

4. The main flaw of the dog is that he is –
   - Ⓐ clumsy
   - Ⓑ jealous
   - Ⓒ rude
   - Ⓓ foolish

The Little Things

Every morning when Patrick woke up he would throw up his arms, let out a yawn, and jump out of bed.

"Up and at 'em," he'd always bellow loudly.

Patrick had his breakfast and then got dressed in his overalls. He strolled out to his garden to tend to his vibrant flowers and gourmet vegetable patch.

Every afternoon, he would bring in new flowers for his wife and some fresh vegetables for dinner. He was always thankful for the meals his wife prepared and she knew the flowers were to show her he appreciated it. She always smiled as she cooked, and Patrick was sure that was why the meals were always delicious.

"It's the little things that make life great," Patrick would always say.

CORE SKILLS PRACTICE

What does the description of Patrick waking up suggest about his personality? Explain your answer.

_____

_____

_____

_____

_____

5   Which phrase from the passage creates a mood of calm?

   Ⓐ   *throw up his arms*

   Ⓑ   *always bellow loudly*

   Ⓒ   *dressed in his overalls*

   Ⓓ   *strolled out to his garden*

6   Patrick would most likely describe his life as –

   Ⓐ   difficult and exhausting

   Ⓑ   exciting and carefree

   Ⓒ   dull and disappointing

   Ⓓ   simple but rewarding

7   What is the main theme of the passage about?

   Ⓐ   Enjoying what you have

   Ⓑ   Growing your own food

   Ⓒ   Having a daily routine

   Ⓓ   Forgetting your troubles

8   The word <u>vibrant</u> suggests that the flowers –

   Ⓐ   move in the breeze

   Ⓑ   are bright and colorful

   Ⓒ   are larger than normal

   Ⓓ   have a pleasant aroma

Directions: Use both passages to answer the following question.

9   What could the dog in the first passage learn from Patrick? Use details from both passages to support your answer.

Reading Comprehension

Set 6

Paired Informational Texts

Instructions

This set contains a pair of passages. Read each passage on its own first. Complete the exercise under each passage. Then complete the questions following each passage.

For each multiple-choice question, fill in the circle for the correct answer. For other types of questions, follow the instructions given. Some of the questions require a written answer. Write your answer on the lines provided.

After reading both passages, you will answer one or more additional questions. You will use information from both passages to answer these questions. Write your answers on the lines provided.

Sugar

Did you know that sugar is a type of crystal? The crystal is edible. It is made out of a fructose molecule and a glucose molecule bonded together to form tiny crystals. It can form large crystals or fine crystals. Large crystals can be crushed or ground down to make finer crystals.

When heated, sugar crystals will begin to melt. They change from solid white particles to a thick liquid. As they are cooked further, they take on a brown color and a nutty flavor develops. This process is called caramelization. This process is often used to make sweets such as toffees and syrups.

Crunchy Toffee

1. Place 1 cup of sugar and ¼ cup of water in a saucepan.
2. Stir as the mixture is heating until all of the sugar has dissolved.
3. Bring the mixture to the boil and continue boiling until the mixture is a dark golden color.
4. Pour the mixture onto a baking tray and allow to cool.
5. Once it is cool, break the toffee into shards.

This crispy toffee is perfect with desserts, on ice cream, or you can even add peanuts to it when it is cooling to make a crunchy peanut toffee.

CORE SKILLS PRACTICE

Locate the information in the passage to answer the questions below.

What is a sugar crystal made of?

_____

What is caramelization?

_____

1. What does the word <u>finer</u> mean as used in the sentence below?

   Large crystals can be crushed or ground down to make finer crystals.

   Ⓐ Nicer

   Ⓑ Sweeter

   Ⓒ Rounder

   Ⓓ Smaller

2. What would you be best to do if you wanted sugar to undergo caramelization?

   Ⓐ Place sugar crystals in boiling water

   Ⓑ Heat sugar crystals in a frying pan

   Ⓒ Crush sugar crystals into finer crystals

   Ⓓ Mix sugar crystals with other ingredients

3. If you were making crunchy peanut toffee, in which step of "Crunchy Toffee" would you add the peanuts?

   Ⓐ Step 2

   Ⓑ Step 3

   Ⓒ Step 4

   Ⓓ Step 5

4. What do you use to determine when to stop boiling the toffee?

   Ⓐ The color of the toffee

   Ⓑ The smell of the toffee

   Ⓒ The thickness of the toffee

   Ⓓ The temperature of the toffee

Sweet Tooth

Did you know that people originally used to chew sugarcane raw? Sugar has been produced since ancient times and originated in India. However, sugar wasn't always so plentiful or so inexpensive. In the early days, honey was used more often than sugar for sweetening food and beverages. At this time, people used to chew on sugarcane, where the sugar was in the form of sugarcane juice. Later, people learned how to turn sugarcane juice into crystallized sugar. This allowed sugar to be stored and transported. This new development was the beginning of sugar becoming more widespread.

At first, sugar remained expensive and was considered a luxury ingredient. Over time, sugarcane crops became more popular and more and more people had access to sugar. It became common to add sugar to foods. Sugar was also one of the first ingredients used, as it is today, to mask the bitter taste of medicine. Today, sugar is a standard ingredient in a whole range of products and most Americans have a store of sugar in the pantry.

CORE SKILLS PRACTICE

How is crystallized sugar different from sugarcane juice? How did this influence sugar's use?

_____

_____

_____

_____

_____

5 The passage states that sugar is used to mask the bitter taste of medicine. Which word could best be used in place of mask?

- Ⓐ Hide
- Ⓑ Sweeten
- Ⓒ Improve
- Ⓓ Destroy

6 Why does the author begin the passage with a question?

- Ⓐ To get readers interested in the topic of the passage
- Ⓑ To show that things have changed since ancient times
- Ⓒ To suggest that readers should research the topic
- Ⓓ To indicate that the information may be incorrect

7 What is the most likely reason honey was used instead of sugar in ancient times?

- Ⓐ Honey tasted sweeter than sugar.
- Ⓑ Honey kept fresh longer than sugar.
- Ⓒ Honey was cheaper than sugar.
- Ⓓ Honey had more uses than sugar.

8 In which sentence does raw mean the same as in the first sentence?

- Ⓐ Clint rubbed the two sticks together until his palms were raw.
- Ⓑ Brian sometimes adds raw eggs to his smoothies.
- Ⓒ The scientists input the raw data into the computer program.
- Ⓓ The first time Jenna sang, her parents knew she had raw talent.

Directions: Use both passages to answer the following question.

9   Describe how the form of sugar changes its properties and how this affects its use. Use details from both passages in your answer.

Reading Comprehension

Set 7

Literary Texts

Instructions

Read each passage. Complete the exercise under each passage.

Then complete the questions following each passage. For each multiple-choice question, fill in the circle for the correct answer. For other types of questions, follow the instructions given. Some of the questions require a written answer. Write your answer on the lines provided.

Gone Fishing

One day Tony and Damien decided to go fishing. Tony had told Damien how he had gone fishing on his uncle's boat once and they had caught huge fish. Tony and Damien were excited about the idea of coming home from their trip carting plenty of massive fish. They got their fishing gear ready at Damien's house. They stopped by the local store to buy some bait and some snacks. On their way, they talked about all the fish they were going to catch.

Tony and Damien arrived at the beach and both cast out their fishing lines. They both waited anxiously for their first catch. There were a few nibbles as the hours went by, but no fish. After a long day of waiting and hoping, Tony let out a sigh. It was starting to get dark and it was time to go home. Tony and Damien didn't catch any fish that day, but they were determined to keep trying. On the way home, they talked about how many fish they might catch the next day.

CORE SKILLS PRACTICE

This story has a third-person point of view. This means it is written by someone who is not part of the story. Now imagine that the story is written from Tony's point of view. Write a paragraph from Tony's point of view describing the day.

_____

_____

_____

_____

_____

_____

1   At the end of the passage, Tony most likely sighs because he is –

Ⓐ   tired

Ⓑ   excited

Ⓒ   angry

Ⓓ   hot

2   What is the main setting of the passage?

Ⓐ   A beach

Ⓑ   Tony's house

Ⓒ   A local store

Ⓓ   A river

3   The main theme of the passage is about –

Ⓐ   being organized

Ⓑ   working hard

Ⓒ   taking your time

Ⓓ   never giving up

4   Which sentence from the passage best shows that the day did not turn out as Tony and Damien thought it would?

Ⓐ   *They got their fishing gear ready at Damien's house.*

Ⓑ   *They stopped by the local store to buy some bait and some snacks.*

Ⓒ   *On their way, they talked about all the fish they were going to catch.*

Ⓓ   *Tony and Damien arrived at the beach and both cast out their fishing lines.*

The Dentist

September 15, 2012

Dear Aunt Sienna,

Today I went to the dentist and had some fillings put in. I had been dreading it all week. I had never had fillings before, and I wasn't sure what to expect. Well, it wasn't the worst thing in the world. It actually didn't take very long and didn't hurt at all! I could definitely think of better things to do though.

When I got home, my mouth felt all weird and tingly. I spent most of the afternoon just reading through comic books and lying in bed. Mom told me that even though it didn't hurt at all, I need to take good care of my teeth. I think maybe I should be eating less candy and brushing more!

Bye for now,

Becky

CORE SKILLS PRACTICE

This passage is a letter. Letters usually follow a set format and have different parts. Complete the table below by identifying each part of the letter and describing its purpose.

Letter Part	Example from the Letter	Purpose of the Part
date line		
greeting		
closing		

English Language Arts, Reading Workbook, Grade 6

1 Becky says that her mouth felt "all weird and tingly." Which word means about the same as weird?

Ⓐ   Stinging

Ⓑ   Sore

Ⓒ   Warm

Ⓓ   Strange

2 How did Becky most likely feel just before getting the fillings in?

Ⓐ   Relieved

Ⓑ   Uneasy

Ⓒ   Thrilled

Ⓓ   Confident

3 What can the reader tell because the passage has a first-person point of view?

Ⓐ   Why Becky went to the dentist

Ⓑ   How Becky felt about going to the dentist

Ⓒ   What Becky did after leaving the dentist

Ⓓ   How long Becky was at the dentist for

4 Which of these themes is best supported by the letter?

Ⓐ   It is better to give than receive.

Ⓑ   There is no time like the present.

Ⓒ   Things are not always as bad as they seem.

Ⓓ   One person's trash is another person's treasure.

The Evil Candide

The princess wished the prince good morrow and went to bed. During the night, the princess was stolen by an evil sorcerer named Candide. Candide was always envious of the prince. He wanted the princess all to himself.

When the prince awoke the next morning to find the princess missing, he knew who had taken her right away. The prince dressed in his finest armor, took up his sword, and galloped off towards Candide's lair to save the princess.

CORE SKILLS PRACTICE

What qualities of an epic does the passage have? In your answer, include what role the prince and Candide each play.

_____

_____

_____

_____

_____

_____

_____

_____

1   Which word means about the same as <u>envious</u>?

   Ⓐ   Afraid

   Ⓑ   Impressed

   Ⓒ   Annoyed

   Ⓓ   Jealous

2   Which words used in the passage suggest that the story takes place a long time ago?

   Ⓐ   *good morrow*

   Ⓑ   *all to himself*

   Ⓒ   *the next morning*

   Ⓓ   *galloped off*

3   What will most likely happen next in the passage?

   Ⓐ   The princess will run away.

   Ⓑ   The prince will save the princess.

   Ⓒ   Candide will take the princess home.

   Ⓓ   The prince will seek out a new princess.

4   The author most likely refers to Candide's home as a "lair" to —

   Ⓐ   show that it is far away

   Ⓑ   indicate that it is grand and expensive

   Ⓒ   suggest that it is a dangerous place

   Ⓓ   foreshadow that there will be a battle

A Quiet Night

Gloria lit the candle on her windowsill and sat on her bed dressed in her white nightgown. She snuggled up under the covers and propped a thick pillow up against the nightstand. She opened up her book and began to read. The mystery novel became more fascinating and she lost herself in the story. She turned page after page as the candle slowly burned down. The candle flickered slightly. Gloria looked over at her clock.

"Ah, bed time," Gloria said, as the hands struck nine o'clock.

She put her book down on her bedside table and blew out the candle. Then she slowly drifted off to sleep.

CORE SKILLS PRACTICE

What is the purpose of the repetition in the sentence below?

> She turned page after page as the candle slowly burned down.

_____

_____

_____

What is the purpose of the phrase "drifted off" in the sentence below?

> Then she slowly drifted off to sleep.

_____

_____

_____

English Language Arts, Reading Workbook, Grade 6

1 Read this sentence from the passage.

> **She snuggled up under the covers and propped a thick pillow up against the nightstand.**

Which word from the sentence suggests that Gloria was comfortable?

- Ⓐ *snuggled*
- Ⓑ *propped*
- Ⓒ *against*
- Ⓓ *nightstand*

2 Which word best describes the mood of the passage?

- Ⓐ Mysterious
- Ⓑ Joyful
- Ⓒ Peaceful
- Ⓓ Gloomy

3 Which detail in the passage is used to represent time passing?

- Ⓐ Gloria lighting the candle
- Ⓑ The candle burning down
- Ⓒ The candle flickering
- Ⓓ Gloria blowing out the candle

4 Which detail suggests that the setting is in the past?

- Ⓐ Gloria reads her book in bed.
- Ⓑ Gloria goes to sleep at nine o'clock.
- Ⓒ Gloria reads by candlelight.
- Ⓓ Gloria is reading a mystery novel.

5 How does the author's choice of words help show that Gloria feels relaxed? Use information from the passage to support your answer.

Reading Comprehension

Set 8

Informational Texts

Instructions

Read each passage. Complete the exercise under each passage.

Then complete the questions following each passage. For each multiple-choice question, fill in the circle for the correct answer. For other types of questions, follow the instructions given. Some of the questions require a written answer. Write your answer on the lines provided.

King of the Jungle

The lion is a member of the Felidae family. The Felidae family includes all cats, which even includes common house cats. The lion is one of the four big cats of the Panthera genus. The other big cats are the tiger, the jaguar, and the leopard. Exceptionally large male lions can weigh over 550 pounds, making them the second largest living cat after the tiger.

Lions can be found in Africa and in northwest India. In the wild, lions usually live for between 10 and 14 years. Lions in captivity have been known to live for over 20 years. The lion is a vulnerable species. It has seen a steady population decline over the last two decades.

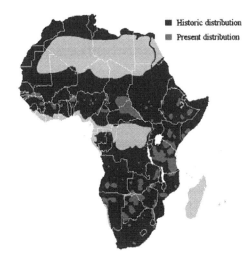

Lions were once found all over Africa. They are now only found in scattered smaller regions.

CORE SKILLS PRACTICE

Describe **one** similarity between lions and tigers and **one** difference between lions and tigers.

_____

_____

_____

_____

1   As it is used in the caption, what does the word <u>scattered</u> show?
   Ⓐ   The regions are away from people.
   Ⓑ   The regions have become smaller.
   Ⓒ   The regions are far apart.
   Ⓓ   The regions have high rainfall.

2   What is the overall tone of the passage?
   Ⓐ   Serious
   Ⓑ   Humorous
   Ⓒ   Regretful
   Ⓓ   Informal

3   Which conclusion is best supported by the passage?
   Ⓐ   There are more lions in captivity than in the wild.
   Ⓑ   Lions tend to live longer in captivity than in the wild.
   Ⓒ   Lions living in captivity lose some of their key skills.
   Ⓓ   Breeding lions in captivity is one way they can be saved.

4   Which idea from the passage does the map best support?
   Ⓐ   Lions are only one of the four big cats.
   Ⓑ   Lions live for between 10 and 14 years.
   Ⓒ   Lions in captivity often live longer.
   Ⓓ   Lion populations have decreased over the years.

Be Prepared

The Scouts is a worldwide youth movement aimed at supporting the physical and mental development of young males. The Scouts was started in 1907 by Robert Baden-Powell, who was a Lieutenant General in the British Army.

During the 1900s, the movement grew to include three different age groups of boys. The Cub Scouts is for boys aged from 7 to 11. The Scouts is for boys aged 11 to 18. The Rover Scouts is for boys aged over 18. In 1910, a similar organization was created for girls. It is known as the Girl Guides. The motto of the Scouts is "Be Prepared." The aim of the Scouts is not just to promote fitness, but to build character. By taking part in a range of activities, members learn important personal skills.

One of the key features of the Scouts is that members earn merit badges as they develop new skills. Some of the badges that can be earned are bird study, rowing, first aid, camping, and public speaking. Once each badge is earned, the patch for the badge can be added to the uniform. It is like a mark that shows what each member has achieved.

CORE SKILLS PRACTICE

Do you think the merit badge system would help motivate members? Explain.

_____

_____

_____

_____

_____

1   Complete the table below using information from the passage.

Age Groups for Boys

Group	Age
Cub Scouts	7 to 11

2   What do the examples of the badges that can be earned best show about being a Scout?

- Ⓐ   You will need to be fit and healthy.
- Ⓑ   You will mainly learn how to help others.
- Ⓒ   You will get to do a range of different things.
- Ⓓ   You will have to work hard to earn each badge.

3   Which word could best replace <u>worldwide</u> in the first sentence?

- Ⓐ   Noteworthy
- Ⓑ   Relevant
- Ⓒ   International
- Ⓓ   Established

4   What is the author's main purpose in the passage?

- Ⓐ   To encourage people to join the Scouts
- Ⓑ   To describe the history of the Scouts
- Ⓒ   To show the importance of fitness to the Scouts
- Ⓓ   To help people choose the right Scouts group to join

Black, Red, and Gold

The modern flag of Germany is a tricolor flag consisting of three horizontal bands of equal size colored black, red, and gold. The flag first appeared in the early nineteenth century. It was originally used by the Frankfurt Parliament and achieved prominence during the 1848 revolution of the German states. During Nazi Germany, the flag's colors were changed to black, white, and red. The flag was restored after World War II. It has been Germany's national flag since 1949.

The modern German flag is made up of three horizontal stripes colored black, red, and gold.

CORE SKILLS PRACTICE

The word *tricolor* contains the Latin root *tri*, which means "three." The word *tricolor* means "having three colors." Complete the table by listing three words that contain the root *tri* and the meaning of each word.

Word	Meaning

1   As it is used in the passage, what does "achieved prominence" mean?
    Ⓐ   Achieved a win
    Ⓑ   Became well-known
    Ⓒ   Won an election
    Ⓓ   Completed a goal

2   How was the flag changed during Nazi Germany?
    Ⓐ   The gold was removed from the flag.
    Ⓑ   The stripes were made smaller.
    Ⓒ   The number of stripes increased to four.
    Ⓓ   The direction of the stripes was altered.

3   How is the passage mainly organized?
    Ⓐ   A solution to a problem is described.
    Ⓑ   Events are described in the order they occurred.
    Ⓒ   Facts are given to support an argument.
    Ⓓ   An event in the past is compared to an event today.

4   Which other title would best help a reader understand the main idea?
    Ⓐ   Modern Life in Germany
    Ⓑ   Changing Times
    Ⓒ   The History of the German Flag
    Ⓓ   Flags of the World

Photosynthesis

The process of turning light energy into chemical energy is called photosynthesis. The process of photosynthesis is how plants get their energy.

Plant leaves and stems have a high amount of a green pigment named chlorophyll contained in them. Light energy from the Sun is absorbed by the chlorophyll. This energy is used to power a reaction between water and carbon dioxide. This reaction produces glucose and oxygen. The plant stores the glucose and uses it for energy. The oxygen is released into the air.

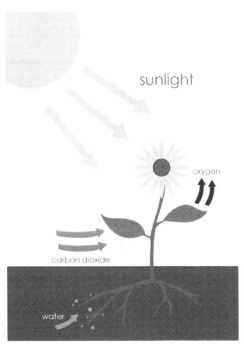

©Wikimedia Commons

CORE SKILLS PRACTICE

Describe the importance of the diagram in the passage. Explain why a diagram benefits this type of passage.

_____

_____

_____

_____

_____

_____

1. Which two words from the passage have the opposite meaning?
   - Ⓐ *light, chemical*
   - Ⓑ *leaves, stems*
   - **●** *absorbed, released*
   - Ⓓ *energy, power*

2. What is the main purpose of the passage?
   - Ⓐ To instruct
   - Ⓑ To entertain
   - Ⓒ To persuade
   - **●** To inform

3. According to the passage, what does the photosynthesis reaction produce?
   - Ⓐ Water
   - Ⓑ Carbon dioxide
   - **●** Glucose
   - Ⓓ Light energy

4. The first sentence of the passage is best described as –
   - Ⓐ a comparison
   - **●** a definition
   - Ⓒ an exaggeration
   - Ⓓ an assumption

5 Describe the process of photosynthesis. Explain how it occurs and why it is important to plants. Use information from the passage to support your answer.

Reading Comprehension

Set 9

Literary and Informational Texts

Instructions

Read each passage. Complete the exercise under each passage.

Then complete the questions following each passage. For each multiple-choice question, fill in the circle for the correct answer. For other types of questions, follow the instructions given. Some of the questions require a written answer. Write your answer on the lines provided.

Flying Scavengers

The Andean Condor is a species of South American bird in the vulture family. It can be found in the Andes mountain range and along the Pacific coast of western South America. The Andean Condor is the largest flying land bird in the Western Hemisphere. Unlike most birds of prey, the male Andean Condor is larger than the female.

©Ester Inbar, Wikimedia Commons

CORE SKILLS PRACTICE

Imagine you want to write a more detailed report about the Andean Condor. What else would you want to include in the report? Write a list of questions you could research and answer in your report.

1. _____

2. _____

3. _____

4. _____

5. _____

English Language Arts, Reading Workbook, Grade 6

1. In what family is the Andean Condor?
   - Ⓐ Hawk
   - Ⓑ Eagle
   - Ⓒ Toucan
   - Ⓓ Vulture

2. Where would this passage most likely be found?
   - Ⓐ In a book of poems
   - Ⓑ In an encyclopedia
   - Ⓒ In a newspaper
   - Ⓓ In a book of short stories

3. What is the main purpose of the passage?
   - Ⓐ To instruct
   - Ⓑ To entertain
   - Ⓒ To persuade
   - Ⓓ To inform

4. The last sentence of the passage is best described as –
   - Ⓐ a comparison
   - Ⓑ a definition
   - Ⓒ an exaggeration
   - Ⓓ an assumption

Artistic Creativity

Every day I enjoy being creative. Some days you will find me painting a portrait. Other days I may be writing a short fiction novel. I even find enjoyment out of sculpting something strange and bizarre into life.

Being artistic is important to me. Every artistic work is a chance to show my own unique style and create something that only I could have created. It is true that a lot of my work is not especially amazing. However, I always have fun challenging myself and experimenting with new ideas.

CORE SKILLS PRACTICE

Think about what the narrator says about being creative. Then think about how you are creative. Write a few paragraphs that argue that it is important to be creative. Include the main benefits of being creative in your argument.

_____

_____

_____

_____

_____

_____

_____

_____

English Language Arts, Reading Workbook, Grade 6

1. Which word means the opposite of <u>bizarre</u>?
   - Ⓐ Ordinary
   - Ⓑ Weird
   - Ⓒ Rare
   - Ⓓ Special

2. Which creative activity is NOT described in the passage?
   - Ⓐ Writing
   - Ⓑ Sculpting
   - Ⓒ Dancing
   - Ⓓ Painting

3. What is the point of view in the passage?
   - Ⓐ First person
   - Ⓑ Second person
   - Ⓒ Third person limited
   - Ⓓ Third person omniscient

4. Which statement would the author of the passage most likely agree with?
   - Ⓐ It takes intense training to develop a talent.
   - Ⓑ It is important to be an individual.
   - Ⓒ Creative tasks should be taken seriously.
   - Ⓓ Sharing your work with other people takes courage.

The Stanley Cup

The Stanley Cup is the most appreciated ice hockey trophy in the world. It is awarded every year to the winner of the National Hockey League (NHL) championships.

Unlike most other sports, a new Stanley Cup is not made each year. Instead, the winning team keeps the trophy until new champions are crowned the next year. This ability to take possession of the trophy makes players appreciate the award even more. Each winning team also has the names of players, coaches, and other team staff engraved on the trophy. This is considered a great honor by all.

The Stanley Cup is the oldest professional sports trophy in North America. It was donated by the Governor General of Canada, Lord Stanley of Preston, in 1892.

CORE SKILLS PRACTICE

What makes the Stanley Cup special? Use at least **two** details from the passage in your answer.

_____
_____
_____
_____
_____
_____

1. In the first sentence, which word could best replace <u>appreciated</u>?
   - Ⓐ Valued
   - Ⓑ Awarded
   - Ⓒ Ancient
   - Ⓓ Curious

2. Why is the last paragraph important to the passage?
   - Ⓐ It shows that ice hockey has been played for a long time.
   - Ⓑ It shows that ice hockey is a national sport.
   - Ⓒ It shows the long history of the trophy.
   - Ⓓ It shows that the trophy is most important to Canadians.

3. Which sentence from the passage is an opinion?
   - Ⓐ *It is awarded every year to the winner of the National Hockey League (NHL) championships.*
   - Ⓑ *This ability to take possession of the trophy makes players appreciate the award even more.*
   - Ⓒ *The Stanley Cup is the oldest professional sports trophy in North America.*
   - Ⓓ *It was donated by the Governor General of Canada, Lord Stanley of Preston, in 1892.*

4. The way that the trophy is engraved with names supports which idea?
   - Ⓐ Learning from those that came before you
   - Ⓑ Always trying to perform better
   - Ⓒ Striving for greatness rather than money or fame
   - Ⓓ Remembering and respecting past achievements

A Special Student

June enjoyed being in school. She enjoyed watching the children play and sometimes sharing their lunches. June enjoyed seeing her friends play skip rope and liked having a nap in the afternoons. June sometimes got to enjoy eating the grass on the football field. June wasn't any ordinary student. June was the school mascot.

Every week, June would enjoy having a class of students milk her. Then she would be let out into the paddock for a graze. If it was warm outside, June would stay in the shelter of a tree or stay in her barn. What June liked best of all, is when the students petted her. There were always plenty of students happy to pat her, so June was a very happy school mascot. The students loved June just as much as she loved them. They enjoyed spending time with her and looking after her.

CORE SKILLS PRACTICE

Why do you think the author does not reveal that June is a cow right away? In your answer, explain the effect this has on the reader.

_____

_____

_____

_____

_____

_____

1. What is the point of view in the passage?
   - Ⓐ First person
   - Ⓑ Second person
   - Ⓒ Third person limited
   - Ⓓ Third person omniscient

2. What happens right after June is milked?
   - Ⓐ The children pat her.
   - Ⓑ She has a nap.
   - Ⓒ She is let out to graze.
   - Ⓓ She is given a bath.

3. What is the first clue in the passage that June is a cow?
   - Ⓐ She watches the children play.
   - Ⓑ She shares the student's lunches.
   - Ⓒ She has a nap in the afternoon.
   - Ⓓ She eats the grass on the football field.

4. Which meaning of the word class is used in the second paragraph?
   - Ⓐ A group of students
   - Ⓑ A set of objects with common qualities
   - Ⓒ Elegance in appearance, actions, or style
   - Ⓓ Excellence in some skill or ability

5   Explain how you can tell that June receives excellent care. Use information from the passage to support your answer.

Reading Comprehension

Set 10

Literary and Informational Texts

Instructions

Read each passage. Complete the exercise under each passage.

Then complete the questions following each passage. For each multiple-choice question, fill in the circle for the correct answer. For other types of questions, follow the instructions given. Some of the questions require a written answer. Write your answer on the lines provided.

Cartoons

Every morning before school, I love to watch cartoons. People say I'm getting too old for cartoons, but I just think that cartoons are funny. My big sister Annie always reminds me that I'm not a kid anymore. But I think anyone can watch cartoons, not just kids.

The jokes are what I like the best. Plus I love watching something that isn't serious at all. You can just let go and enjoy the show! I don't think I'll ever stop watching cartoons, even if other people think I'm too old for them.

CORE SKILLS PRACTICE

Some people think that cartoons are silly. Other people, like the speaker in the passage, think that cartoons are entertaining. What is your opinion of cartoons?

_____

_____

_____

_____

_____

_____

English Language Arts, Reading Workbook, Grade 6

1 The narrator says that "you can just let go and enjoy the show!" What does the phrase "let go" refer to?

- Ⓐ Sitting
- Ⓑ Relaxing
- Ⓒ Waiting
- Ⓓ Stopping

2 Which sentence from the passage best shows the main idea?

- Ⓐ *My big sister Annie always reminds me that I'm not a kid anymore.*
- Ⓑ *The jokes are what I like the best.*
- Ⓒ *Plus I love watching something that isn't serious at all.*
- Ⓓ *I don't think I'll ever stop watching cartoons, even if other people think I'm too old for them.*

3 What is the second paragraph mostly about?

- Ⓐ Why the narrator likes cartoons
- Ⓑ How the narrator is too old for cartoons
- Ⓒ When the narrator likes to watch cartoons
- Ⓓ What other people think of cartoons

4 Which of these words best describes the tone of the passage?

- Ⓐ Chatty
- Ⓑ Proud
- Ⓒ Demanding
- Ⓓ Mischievous

Troy McClure

Troy McClure is a reoccurring character in the popular television animation *The Simpsons*. He was created by writer Mike Reiss. The character was originally based on B-movie actors Troy Donahue and Doug McClure. Troy McClure was voiced by Phil Hartman, who died in 1998. Hartman's death led to the character being retired. It would have been possible to find someone else to be the voice of the character, but the show's producers decided to retire the character instead.

Troy McClure made his final appearance in the tenth season episode titled "Bart the Mother" in late 1989. It was a sad loss for a character that was much-loved by fans. Even though he played a relatively minor role in the show's plot, he is remembered well by fans and remains one of the show's most popular characters.

CORE SKILLS PRACTICE

You can often guess how authors feel about a topic by what they say, what tone they use, and what words they use. How do you think the author feels about the character Troy McClure being retired? Use details from the passage to support your answer.

_____

_____

_____

_____

_____

1. In the first sentence, what does the word <u>reoccurring</u> mean?
   - Ⓐ Occurring again
   - Ⓑ No longer occurring
   - Ⓒ Occurring once
   - Ⓓ Occurring annually

2. Who was Troy McClure named after?
   - Ⓐ The creator of *The Simpsons*
   - Ⓑ The person who was his voice
   - Ⓒ Two B-movie actors
   - Ⓓ Two famous cartoonists

3. Why was the character Troy McClure retired?
   - Ⓐ He was no longer useful in the show.
   - Ⓑ The person who provided his voice died.
   - Ⓒ He was taking the focus off the main characters.
   - Ⓓ He had been appearing in the show too often.

4. In which sentence does <u>plot</u> mean the same as in the last sentence?
   - Ⓐ The novel's <u>plot</u> has a surprising twist at the end.
   - Ⓑ It's a good idea to rake a <u>plot</u> before putting in new plants.
   - Ⓒ We added a <u>plot</u> to our report to show our findings clearly.
   - Ⓓ Kendra came up with a clever <u>plot</u> to trick Jason.

The Park

Dear Diary,

Today Mom and I went for a walk in the park after school. The park is such a pretty and peaceful place with all of those trees, flowers, and birds. We saw people having picnics, and some kids rowing boats on the lake. Some people were also feeding bread to the ducks. Others were just lazing around in the sun or reading books.

We saw one man who was painted in silver paint. He was standing completely still and changing his pose every few minutes. While he was still, he looked exactly like a statue! It was pretty amazing to watch. Mom and I took a photo in front of him. We said goodbye and left some change in his tip jar. What a great afternoon!

Kira

CORE SKILLS PRACTICE

You can make inferences by using information in a passage as well as your own prior knowledge. Answer the question below by making an inference.

Why do you think the man in the park was pretending to be a statue?

_____

_____

_____

_____

_____

English Language Arts, Reading Workbook, Grade 6

1. As it is used below, which word means the opposite of <u>still</u>?

   He was standing completely still and changing his pose every few minutes.

   Ⓐ Moving

   Ⓑ Noisy

   Ⓒ Silent

   Ⓓ Motionless

2. Describe **four** things that Kira saw people doing in the park.

Things that Kira Saw People Doing in the Park	
1)	3)
2)	4)

3. How is the second paragraph different from the first?

   Ⓐ It tells the main reason that Kira and her mother visited the park.

   Ⓑ It supports the idea that the park is pretty and peaceful.

   Ⓒ It describes one of the things that Kira saw in detail.

   Ⓓ It explains why Kira and her mother left the park.

4. What does the photograph in the passage represent?

   Ⓐ Why Kira visited the park

   Ⓑ How Kira's mother uses the park

   Ⓒ One thing Kira saw people doing in the park

   Ⓓ What Kira likes most about the park

Breaking In

Today, Apple is a success in the personal computer market. It offers a range of effective and attractive products. But it wasn't always that way. Apple had to struggle to break into the market.

At the time, IBM was the leader in the market. Then Apple introduced the iMac G3 in 1998. The iMac G3 was one of the first commercial successes for Apple. Previous to the iMac, Apple saw only limited success with its earlier desktop models.

The iMac G3 came after new Apple CEO Steve Jobs decided to trim Apple's product line. He decided to relaunch with a focus on simplicity. It was a bold move and an effective one. The striking design of the iMac was just one of the reasons it was special.

The iMac G3 was unlike any computer that had been seen. The computer parts were no longer in a separate case, but were part of the monitor. The computer now looked better and took up less space. It was originally released in blue, but other bright colors were soon added. The styling was an immediate hit.

CORE SKILLS PRACTICE

What lesson does the passage have about taking a chance and being different?

_____

_____

_____

_____

1. The passage states that Steve Jobs decided to trim Apple's product line. The word <u>trim</u> is used to show that Steve Jobs –

   Ⓐ made each product smaller

   Ⓑ reduced the number of products

   Ⓒ decreased the weight of the products

   Ⓓ made the products look more attractive

2. The author probably wrote this passage to –

   Ⓐ encourage people to buy Apple products

   Ⓑ describe a turning point for a company

   Ⓒ analyze the sales techniques of a computer company

   Ⓓ tell about the life of Steve Jobs

3. Which sentence from the passage is a fact?

   Ⓐ *It offers a range of effective and attractive products.*

   Ⓑ *Then Apple introduced the iMac G3 in 1998.*

   Ⓒ *It was a bold move and an effective one.*

   Ⓓ *The striking design of the iMac was just one of the reasons it was special.*

4. In which sentence does <u>hit</u> mean the same as in the caption?

   Ⓐ The song we sang at the talent contest was a <u>hit</u> with everyone.

   Ⓑ I was trying to <u>hit</u> the nail, but I missed and hurt my thumb.

   Ⓒ I walked out with my bat determined to <u>hit</u> the ball out of the park.

   Ⓓ It has been hard to teach my little sister not to <u>hit</u> or kick other kids.

5. What made the iMac G3 so successful? Give at least **two** reasons in your answer. Use information from the passage to support your answer.

Reading Comprehension

Set 11

Paired Literary Texts

Instructions

This set contains a pair of passages. Read each passage on its own first. Complete the exercise under each passage. Then complete the questions following each passage.

For each multiple-choice question, fill in the circle for the correct answer. For other types of questions, follow the instructions given. Some of the questions require a written answer. Write your answer on the lines provided.

After reading both passages, you will answer one or more additional questions. You will use information from both passages to answer these questions. Write your answers on the lines provided.

The Astronomer

An astronomer used to go out at night to observe the stars. One evening, he was wandering around town with his eyes fixed on the sky. He suddenly tripped and fell into a well. He sat there and groaned about his sores and bruises and cried for help. He pummeled his fists against the well. He looked up and all he could see were the stars. The twinkling stars looked back down on him and laughed.

The astronomer's friend finally heard his cries and made his way over to the well. After hearing the astronomer's story of how he fell, he simply shook his head.

"Old friend, in striving to see into the heavens, you don't manage to see what is on the earth," the friend said.

CORE SKILLS PRACTICE

The author does not state how the astronomer feels about being stuck in the well, but you can make an inference about how he feels based on the details given. On the lines below, describe how you think the astronomer feels and how you can tell.

_____

_____

_____

_____

_____

1   In the sentence below, the word <u>fixed</u> describes which action?

    One evening, he was wandering around town with his eyes fixed on the sky.

    Ⓐ   Staring

    Ⓑ   Blinking

    Ⓒ   Glancing

    Ⓓ   Glaring

2   Which sentence represents the astronomer suffering because of his error?

    Ⓐ   *One evening, he was wandering around town with his eyes fixed on the sky.*

    Ⓑ   *He sat there and groaned about his sores and bruises and cried for help.*

    Ⓒ   *He looked up and all he could see were the stars.*

    Ⓓ   *The twinkling stars looked back down on him and laughed.*

3   The main theme of the passage is about –

    Ⓐ   having an interesting hobby

    Ⓑ   not being afraid to ask for help

    Ⓒ   being careful at all times

    Ⓓ   not focusing too much on one thing

4   What is the main purpose of the last paragraph of the passage?

    Ⓐ   To show that the astronomer has changed

    Ⓑ   To show how passionate the astronomer is

    Ⓒ   To show that the story has a happy ending

    Ⓓ   To show the moral lesson of the story

Drummer Boy

Tap-tap-tap, ratta-tat-tat. Tim used his two pencils on his school desk like drumsticks. He hummed his favorite tune as he enjoyed daydreaming. A few students glared at him, but Tim didn't even notice. He just kept playing his song, while imagining he was on stage in front of hoards of screaming fans. Tim's drumming became louder and louder as he continued playing for the imaginary crowd. The classroom became silent as everyone stared at Tim. In his mind, the silence was the crowd waiting for his final drum solo. Mr. Paulson turned around from writing on the board.

"Tim! Would you cut that out?" Mr. Paulson hollered.

Tim nearly jumped out of his chair as he came back to reality. He looked around the room, and realized that all eyes were on him. Unlike in his daydream, they were not marveling at his musical talent.

"Sorry about that, sir!" Tim said as all the other kids chuckled a little.

Mr. Paulson went back to writing on the board. Tim opened his notebook and wrote in it. *One day I'm going to be in a band*, he wrote.

CORE SKILLS PRACTICE

In the first paragraph, how can you tell that Tim gets lost in his daydream?

_____

_____

_____

_____

5   What does the phrase "cut that out" mean?

"Tim! Would you cut that out?" Mr. Paulson hollered.

- Ⓐ   Scratch it
- Ⓑ   Remove it
- Ⓒ   Stop it
- Ⓓ   Decrease it

6   Which word best describes Tim while he is in class?
- Ⓐ   Distracted
- Ⓑ   Anxious
- Ⓒ   Relaxed
- Ⓓ   Annoyed

7   Why does the author have text in italics in the last sentence?
- Ⓐ   To suggest that the text was spoken
- Ⓑ   To show that it is a flashback
- Ⓒ   To emphasize the main point
- Ⓓ   To indicate written text

8   Why does the author say that Tim "nearly jumped out of his chair" when Mr. Paulson spoke?
- Ⓐ   To highlight how embarrassed Tim felt
- Ⓑ   To emphasize how annoyed the teacher was
- Ⓒ   To show that Tim was startled
- Ⓓ   To suggest that Tim was really enjoying his drumming

Directions: Use both passages to answer the following question.

9   How is the lesson that the astronomer and Tim learn similar? Use details from both passages to support your answer.

Reading Comprehension

Set 12

Paired Informational Texts

Instructions

This set contains a pair of passages. Read each passage on its own first. Complete the exercise under each passage. Then complete the questions following each passage.

For each multiple-choice question, fill in the circle for the correct answer. For other types of questions, follow the instructions given. Some of the questions require a written answer. Write your answer on the lines provided.

After reading both passages, you will answer one or more additional questions. You will use information from both passages to answer these questions. Write your answers on the lines provided.

Radiohead

Radiohead are an alternative rock band from Oxfordshire in England. They are a five piece band that first formed in 1985. They formed while the members were attending private school together. The band continued to practice and perform as the members completed college. It was only after years of practice that the band was signed to a record label.

Radiohead released their first single, titled "Creep," in 1992. The song was initially unsuccessful. However, it became a hit after the release of their debut album, titled *Pablo Honey*, in 1993. Radiohead's first six albums had sold more than 25 million copies by 2007. They continued to produce music and tour and by 2011, they had released their eighth album. In 2005, they had the honor of being named number 73 on a list of the greatest musical artists of all time.

CORE SKILLS PRACTICE

Like many bands, Radiohead struggled for years before achieving success. Many other bands continue to struggle and never have a big break. Do you think it is still worthwhile for bands to keep trying? Explain your answer.

_____

_____

_____

_____

_____

_____

English Language Arts, Reading Workbook, Grade 6

1. Why does the author most likely include the sentence below?

   Radiohead's first six albums had sold more than 25 million copies by 2007.

   - Ⓐ To show that Radiohead stayed together a long time
   - Ⓑ To show the reader that Radiohead achieved success
   - Ⓒ To show that Radiohead's first single was a hit
   - Ⓓ To show the reader the style of Radiohead's music

2. How is the passage mainly organized?
   - Ⓐ A solution to a problem is described.
   - Ⓑ Events are described in the order they occurred.
   - Ⓒ Facts are given to support an argument.
   - Ⓓ An event in the past is compared to an event today.

3. What is the main purpose of the passage?
   - Ⓐ To give details about a successful band
   - Ⓑ To encourage people to listen to music
   - Ⓒ To argue that bands are better than solo artists
   - Ⓓ To explain why a band was popular

4. In the first paragraph, the word <u>signed</u> means that the record company –
   - Ⓐ noticed the band
   - Ⓑ changed the band's name
   - Ⓒ offered the band advice
   - Ⓓ gave the band a deal

Like a Rolling Stone

The Rolling Stones are one of the most successful rock and roll groups ever. After forming in London in April 1962, The Rolling Stones have stood the test of time. They have released over 30 successful albums, and have sold over 200 million albums worldwide.

They are even still playing today, led by original vocalist Mick Jagger and guitarist Keith Richards. Among The Rolling Stones' many popular songs are "You Can't Always Get What You Want" and "Paint It, Black." Many of their songs have also been covered by other bands and artists.

In this picture from 1965, the members of The Rolling Stones were in their early twenties. In 2006, the band toured and performed all over America. Amazingly, the band members were in their sixties. This didn't stop them from putting on a great show.

CORE SKILLS PRACTICE

How do you think the author of the passage feels about The Rolling Stones? Explain how the author's feelings show in the passage.

_____

_____

_____

_____

_____

5   A vocalist is most likely –

  Ⓐ   the person who formed a band

  Ⓑ   the singer of a band

  Ⓒ   the oldest member of a band

  Ⓓ   the drummer of a band

6   Which detail best supports the idea that The Rolling Stones have stood the test of time?

  Ⓐ   They first formed in London.

  Ⓑ   They have many popular songs.

  Ⓒ   They are still playing today.

  Ⓓ   Other bands have covered their songs.

7   What is the main purpose of the passage?

  Ⓐ   To instruct

  Ⓑ   To entertain

  Ⓒ   To inform

  Ⓓ   To persuade

8   The author would probably describe the band touring when the members were in their sixties as –

  Ⓐ   ordinary

  Ⓑ   ridiculous

  Ⓒ   outrageous

  Ⓓ   admirable

Directions: Use both passages to answer the following questions.

9   Describe how the two passages present information in similar ways.

_____

_____

_____

_____

_____

10 How can you tell that The Rolling Stones are more successful than Radiohead? Use details from both passages to support your answer.

_____

_____

_____

_____

_____

_____

ANSWER KEY

Skills and State Standards

The *Massachusetts Curriculum Frameworks* are a set of standards that describe what students are expected to know. Student learning throughout the year is based on these standards, and all the questions on the state tests assess these standards. In 2017, new *Massachusetts Curriculum Frameworks* were introduced. Beginning in spring 2018, the MCAS tests will assess the 2017 *Massachusetts Curriculum Frameworks*. All the exercises and questions in this book cover the skills listed in the 2017 *Massachusetts Curriculum Frameworks*.

Core Skills Practice

Each passage includes an exercise focused on one key skill described in the state standards. The answer key identifies the core skill covered by each exercise, and describes what to look for in the student's response.

Reading Standards

The reading standards are divided into the following two areas:

- Reading Standards for Literature
- Reading Standards for Informational Text

Within each of these areas, there are standards that describe specific skills the student should have. The answer key on the following pages lists the standard assessed by each question. The skill listed can be used to identify a student's areas of strength and weakness, so revision and instruction can be targeted accordingly.

Scoring Written Response Questions

This workbook includes short response and essay questions. The answer key gives guidance on how to score these questions. Use the criteria listed as a guide to scoring these questions, and as a guide for giving the student advice on how to improve an answer.

English Language Arts, Reading Workbook, Grade 6

Set 1: Literary Texts

Snowed In

Core Skills Practice

Core skill: Describe how the plot of a particular story, poem, or drama unfolds in a series of episodes as well as how the characters respond or change as the plot moves toward a resolution.
Answer: The student should explain that the storm caused the loss of the communication tower, which caused Dr. Nord to be stuck in the research bunker waiting for rescue.

Question	Answer	Reading Standard
1	B	Determine the meaning of words and phrases as they are used in a text, including figurative and connotative meanings; analyze the impact of specific word choices, including those that create repeated sounds and rhythms in poetry, on meaning, tone, or mood.
2	C	Describe how the plot of a particular story, poem, or drama unfolds in a series of episodes as well as how the characters respond or change as the plot moves toward a resolution.
3	A	Cite textual evidence to support analysis of what a text states explicitly as well as inferences drawn from the text, quoting or paraphrasing as appropriate.
4	A	Compare and contrast the experience of reading a story, drama, or poem to that of listening to or viewing the same text.

The Miner

Core Skills Practice

Core skill: Explain how an author develops the point of view of the narrator or speaker in a text.
Answer: The student should write a paragraph describing the miner's search for gold. The narrative should be written in first-person point of view and include details of the miner's thoughts and feelings.

Question	Answer	Reading Standard
1	A	Determine the meaning of words and phrases as they are used in a text, including figurative and connotative meanings; analyze the impact of specific word choices, including those that create repeated sounds and rhythms in poetry, on meaning, tone, or mood.
2	B	Cite textual evidence to support analysis of what a text states explicitly as well as inferences drawn from the text, quoting or paraphrasing as appropriate.
3	C	Determine the meaning of words and phrases as they are used in a text, including figurative and connotative meanings; analyze the impact of specific word choices, including those that create repeated sounds and rhythms in poetry, on meaning, tone, or mood.
4	D	Analyze how a particular sentence, chapter, scene, or stanza fits into the overall structure of a text and contributes to the development of the theme, setting, or plot.

What Caterpillars Do

Core Skills Practice

Core skill: Determine a theme or central idea of a text and how it is conveyed through particular details; provide a summary of a text distinct from personal opinions or judgments.

Answer: The student should identify the theme as being about the way that living things have special abilities or as being about accepting the special things that you can do. The student should describe how the poet communicates the theme by describing how little caterpillars can do, but then describing how they have the unique ability to turn into a butterfly.

Question	Answer	Reading Standard
1	D	Explain how an author develops the point of view of the narrator or speaker in a text.
2	B	Analyze how a particular sentence, chapter, scene, or stanza fits into the overall structure of a text and contributes to the development of the theme, setting, or plot.
3	D	Analyze how a particular sentence, chapter, scene, or stanza fits into the overall structure of a text and contributes to the development of the theme, setting, or plot.
4	C	Determine a theme or central idea of a text and how it is conveyed through particular details; provide a summary of a text distinct from personal opinions or judgments.

Flying High

Core Skills Practice

Core skill: Cite textual evidence to support analysis of what a text states explicitly as well as inferences drawn from the text, quoting or paraphrasing as appropriate.

Answer: The student should describe how he or she would feel about living near an airport. Students should clearly explain either the problems of living near an airport, or the positive aspects of living near an airport.

Question	Answer	Reading Standard
1	C	Determine the meaning of words and phrases as they are used in a text, including figurative and connotative meanings; analyze the impact of specific word choices, including those that create repeated sounds and rhythms in poetry, on meaning, tone, or mood.
2	D	Determine a theme or central idea of a text and how it is conveyed through particular details; provide a summary of a text distinct from personal opinions or judgments.
3	D	Cite textual evidence to support analysis of what a text states explicitly as well as inferences drawn from the text, quoting or paraphrasing as appropriate.
4	D	Explain how an author develops the point of view of the narrator or speaker in a text.
5	See Below	Determine the meaning of words and phrases as they are used in a text, including figurative and connotative meanings; analyze the impact of specific word choices, including those that create repeated sounds and rhythms in poetry, on meaning, tone, or mood.

Give a score of 0, 1, 2, 3, or 4 based on how well the answer meets the criteria listed.
- It should identify that the simile is when the author describes the airplanes as soaring overhead like giant metallic birds.
- It should provide a fully-supported explanation of why the author used the simile.
- It should use relevant details from the passage.
- It should be well-organized, clear, and easy to understand.

English Language Arts, Reading Workbook, Grade 6

Set 2: Informational Texts

Brain in a Bottle

Core Skills Practice

Core skill: Analyze in detail how a key individual, event, or idea is introduced, illustrated, and elaborated in a text.
Answer: The student should list the two differences below.
 1. The parietal lobe was larger than normal.
 2. The parietal lobe was not separated into two compartments.

Question	Answer	Reading Standard
1	D	Determine the meaning of words and phrases as they are used in a text, including figurative, connotative, and technical meanings; explain how word choice affects meaning and tone.
2	A	Analyze how a particular sentence, paragraph, chapter, section, or text feature fits into the overall structure of a text and contributes to the development of the ideas.
3	A	Determine a text's central idea(s) and how particular details help convey the idea(s); provide a summary of a text distinct from personal opinions or judgments.
4	B	Analyze in detail how a key individual, event, or idea is introduced, illustrated, and elaborated in a text.

Hillary Clinton

Core Skills Practice

Core skill: Compare and contrast one author's presentation of events with that of another.
Answer: The student should provide a reasonable description of how a memoir would be different from the passage. The answer may refer to how the memoir would describe events from Hillary Clinton's point of view, how the memoir would be more personal, or how the memoir would be less formal.

Question	Answer	Reading Standard
1	D	Determine the meaning of words and phrases as they are used in a text, including figurative, connotative, and technical meanings; explain how word choice affects meaning and tone.
2	A	Compare and contrast one author's presentation of events with that of another.
3	B	Integrate information presented in different media or formats as well as in words to develop a coherent understanding of a topic or issue.
4	A	Determine a text's central idea(s) and how particular details help convey the idea(s); provide a summary of a text distinct from personal opinions or judgments.

Antique Map

Core Skills Practice

Core skill: Integrate information presented in different media or formats as well as in words to develop a coherent understanding of a topic or issue.

Answer: The student should list how the map is darkened or yellowed to look older and how the edges of the map are marked and torn.

Question	Answer	Reading Standard
1	C	Analyze how a particular sentence, paragraph, chapter, section, or text feature fits into the overall structure of a text and contributes to the development of the ideas.
2	B	Integrate information presented in different media or formats as well as in words to develop a coherent understanding of a topic or issue.
3	D	Cite textual evidence to support analysis of what a text states explicitly as well as inferences drawn from the text, quoting or paraphrasing as appropriate.
4	C	Determine the meaning of words and phrases as they are used in a text, including figurative, connotative, and technical meanings; explain how word choice affects meaning and tone.

Defeat at Waterloo

Core Skills Practice

Core skill: Cite textual evidence to support analysis of what a text states explicitly as well as inferences drawn from the text, quoting or paraphrasing as appropriate.

Answer: The student should infer that Napoleon's French Army were outnumbered. The answer should use the detail given about the "enormous coalition of European forces" to support the answer.

Question	Answer	Reading Standard
1	D	Determine the meaning of words and phrases as they are used in a text, including figurative, connotative, and technical meanings; explain how word choice affects meaning and tone.
2	B	Determine an author's point of view or purpose in a text and explain how it is conveyed in the text.
3	B	Analyze how a particular sentence, paragraph, chapter, section, or text feature fits into the overall structure of a text and contributes to the development of the ideas.
4	A	Integrate information presented in different media or formats as well as in words to develop a coherent understanding of a topic or issue.
5	See Below	Determine a text's central idea(s) and how particular details help convey the idea(s); provide a summary of a text distinct from personal opinions or judgments.

Give a score of 0, 1, 2, 3, or 4 based on how well the answer meets the criteria listed.
- It should state whether or not Napoleon Bonaparte was a successful military leader.
- It should provide a fully-supported explanation of why the student drew this conclusion.
- It should use relevant details from the passage.
- It should be well-organized, clear, and easy to understand.

Set 3: Literary and Informational Texts

Belarus

Core Skills Practice

Core skill: Determine a text's central idea(s) and how particular details help convey the idea(s); provide a summary of a text distinct from personal opinions or judgments.

Answer: The student should list two ways that Belarus is still connected to Russia. The student may describe how Belarus borders Russia, has Russian as one of its official languages, exports goods to Russia, or imports goods from Russia.

Question	Answer	Reading Standard
1	A	Integrate information presented in different media or formats as well as in words to develop a coherent understanding of a topic or issue.
2	B	Cite textual evidence to support analysis of what a text states explicitly as well as inferences drawn from the text, quoting or paraphrasing as appropriate.
3	C	Compare and contrast one author's presentation of events with that of another.
4	A	Determine the meaning of words and phrases as they are used in a text, including figurative, connotative, and technical meanings; explain how word choice affects meaning and tone.

Magnetic North

Core Skills Practice

Core skill: Trace and evaluate the argument and specific claims in a text, distinguishing claims that are supported by reasons and evidence from claims that are not.

Answer: The student should give a correct explanation as to why compasses are not as important to sailors as they once were. The answer should refer to how compasses have been replaced by more modern technologies that making finding the direction and navigating easier.

Question	Answer	Reading Standard
1	D	Cite textual evidence to support analysis of what a text states explicitly as well as inferences drawn from the text, quoting or paraphrasing as appropriate.
2	B	Integrate information presented in different media or formats as well as in words to develop a coherent understanding of a topic or issue.
3	A	Analyze how a particular sentence, paragraph, chapter, section, or text feature fits into the overall structure of a text and contributes to the development of the ideas.
4	A	Determine the meaning of words and phrases as they are used in a text, including figurative, connotative, and technical meanings; explain how word choice affects meaning and tone.

Hide and Seek

Core Skills Practice

Core skill: Describe how the plot of a particular story, poem, or drama unfolds in a series of episodes as well as how the characters respond or change as the plot moves toward a resolution.

Answer: The student should explain that it is ironic that Jeremy plans to scare Vanessa, but then is scared by Vanessa instead.

Question	Answer	Reading Standard
1	A	Determine the meaning of words and phrases as they are used in a text, including figurative and connotative meanings; analyze the impact of specific word choices, including those that create repeated sounds and rhythms in poetry, on meaning, tone, or mood.
2	D	Determine the meaning of words and phrases as they are used in a text, including figurative and connotative meanings; analyze the impact of specific word choices, including those that create repeated sounds and rhythms in poetry, on meaning, tone, or mood.
3	C	Describe how the plot of a particular story, poem, or drama unfolds in a series of episodes as well as how the characters respond or change as the plot moves toward a resolution.
4	B	Cite textual evidence to support analysis of what a text states explicitly as well as inferences drawn from the text, quoting or paraphrasing as appropriate.

Danny's Homework

Core Skills Practice

Core skill: Explain how an author develops the point of view of the narrator or speaker in a text.

Answer: The student should identify details that show that Danny was worried about losing his work. The student may describe Danny's actions, such as pressing the power button repeatedly and running to plug the laptop in. The student may also refer to how Danny sighs when he sees that his work was saved, which shows his relief.

Question	Answer	Reading Standard
1	D	Determine the meaning of words and phrases as they are used in a text, including figurative and connotative meanings; analyze the impact of specific word choices, including those that create repeated sounds and rhythms in poetry, on meaning, tone, or mood.
2	B	Describe how the plot of a particular story, poem, or drama unfolds in a series of episodes as well as how the characters respond or change as the plot moves toward a resolution.
3	A	Explain how an author develops the point of view of the narrator or speaker in a text.
4	A	Determine the meaning of words and phrases as they are used in a text, including figurative and connotative meanings; analyze the impact of specific word choices, including those that create repeated sounds and rhythms in poetry, on meaning, tone, or mood.
5	See Below	Cite textual evidence to support analysis of what a text states explicitly as well as inferences drawn from the text, quoting or paraphrasing as appropriate.

Give a score of 0, 1, 2, 3, or 4 based on how well the answer meets the criteria listed.
- It should state a prediction of what Danny will do the next time he uses his laptop to do his homework.
- It should provide a fully-supported explanation of why the student made this prediction.
- It should use relevant details from the passage, and may also include prior knowledge.
- It should be well-organized, clear, and easy to understand.

English Language Arts, Reading Workbook, Grade 6

Set 4: Literary and Informational Texts

Ruler of Macedon

Core Skills Practice

Core skill: Trace and evaluate the argument and specific claims in a text, distinguishing claims that are supported by reasons and evidence from claims that are not.

Answer: The student should identify details that show that Alexander the Great was a noteworthy king. The supporting details include that he created one of the largest empires by the age of 30, that he caused the fall of a Persian king, that his achievements are still taught today, or that he is known as Alexander "the Great."

Question	Answer	Reading Standard
1	C	Determine the meaning of words and phrases as they are used in a text, including figurative, connotative, and technical meanings; explain how word choice affects meaning and tone.
2	D	Analyze in detail how a key individual, event, or idea is introduced, illustrated, and elaborated in a text.
3	B	Compare and contrast one author's presentation of events with that of another.
4	B	Determine the meaning of words and phrases as they are used in a text, including figurative, connotative, and technical meanings; explain how word choice affects meaning and tone.

Bananas

Core Skills Practice

Core skill: Cite textual evidence to support analysis of what a text states explicitly as well as inferences drawn from the text, quoting or paraphrasing as appropriate.

Answer: The student should give details that suggest that Jacky will change how she eats bananas. The answer could refer to how she says she learned that she's been doing it wrong, how she says the new way is easy, how she says she was impressed, or how she says that Dad was right or that monkeys are smarter than her.

Question	Answer	Reading Standard
1	B	Determine the meaning of words and phrases as they are used in a text, including figurative, connotative, and technical meanings; explain how word choice affects meaning and tone.
2	B	Cite textual evidence to support analysis of what a text states explicitly as well as inferences drawn from the text, quoting or paraphrasing as appropriate.
3	C	Analyze in detail how a key individual, event, or idea is introduced, illustrated, and elaborated in a text.
4	B	Determine the meaning of words and phrases as they are used in a text, including figurative, connotative, and technical meanings; explain how word choice affects meaning and tone.

English Language Arts, Reading Workbook, Grade 6

The Human Skeleton

Core Skills Practice

Core skill: Determine the meaning of words and phrases as they are used in a text, including figurative, connotative, and technical meanings.

Answer: The student should write a valid definition of each word. Examples are given below.
fused: joined together
brittle: weak or able to break easily
fracture: a break in a bone
sufficient: enough

Question	Answer	Reading Standard
1	D	Determine the meaning of words and phrases as they are used in a text, including figurative, connotative, and technical meanings; explain how word choice affects meaning and tone.
2	Protecting vital organs Generating blood cells Storing minerals	Determine a text's central idea(s) and how particular details help convey the idea(s); provide a summary of a text distinct from personal opinions or judgments.
3	B	Cite textual evidence to support analysis of what a text states explicitly as well as inferences drawn from the text, quoting or paraphrasing as appropriate.
4	C	Analyze how a particular sentence, paragraph, chapter, section, or text feature fits into the overall structure of a text and contributes to the development of the ideas.

The Desert Oasis

Core Skills Practice

Core skill: Compare and contrast texts in different forms or genres in terms of their approaches to similar themes and topics.

Answer: The student should describe how the passage is like a quest. The student may identify that Serian is on a difficult journey, is battling forces of nature, has only himself to rely on, or is on a mission to reach a new land.

Question	Answer	Reading Standard
1	B	Compare and contrast texts in different forms or genres in terms of their approaches to similar themes and topics.
2	B	Describe how the plot of a particular story, poem, or drama unfolds in a series of episodes as well as how the characters respond or change as the plot moves toward a resolution.
3	B	Cite textual evidence to support analysis of what a text states explicitly as well as inferences drawn from the text, quoting or paraphrasing as appropriate.
4	C	Compare and contrast the experience of reading a story, drama, or poem to that of listening to or viewing the same text.
5	See Below	Describe how the plot of a particular story, poem, or drama unfolds in a series of episodes as well as how the characters respond or change as the plot moves toward a resolution.

Give a score of 0, 1, 2, 3, or 4 based on how well the answer meets the criteria listed.
- It should state how Serian feels when he sees the oasis.
- The answer should describe Serian as feeling pleased, relieved, determined, or overjoyed.
- It should provide a fully-supported explanation of why the student believes this.
- The explanation may refer to how he feels in the first paragraph, how he acts when he first sees the oasis, how he smiles as he walks toward the oasis, or how he will finally be able to rest at the oasis.
- It should be well-organized, clear, and easy to understand.

English Language Arts, Reading Workbook, Grade 6

Set 5: Paired Literary Texts

The Dog and the River/The Little Things

Core Skills Practice
Core skill: Compare and contrast texts in different forms or genres in terms of their approaches to similar themes and topics.
Answer: The student should identify that the events are not realistic. The student may describe how the dog has thoughts and feelings as if it is human. The student may also describe how a dog would probably not do what the dog in the passage does, and may refer to how the events are made up to make a point.

Core Skills Practice
Core skill: Analyze how a particular sentence, chapter, scene, or stanza fits into the overall structure of a text and contributes to the development of the theme, setting, or plot.
Answer: The student should identify that the description of Patrick waking up shows that he is positive, happy, or enthusiastic. The answer may refer to how he throws up his arms, jumps out of bed, or bellows loudly.

Question	Answer	Reading Standard
1	D	Compare and contrast texts in different forms or genres in terms of their approaches to similar themes and topics.
2	B	Determine a theme or central idea of a text and how it is conveyed through particular details; provide a summary of a text distinct from personal opinions or judgments.
3	A	Describe how the plot of a particular story, poem, or drama unfolds in a series of episodes as well as how the characters respond or change as the plot moves toward a resolution.
4	B	Determine a theme or central idea of a text and how it is conveyed through particular details; provide a summary of a text distinct from personal opinions or judgments.
5	D	Determine the meaning of words and phrases as they are used in a text, including figurative and connotative meanings; analyze the impact of specific word choices, including those that create repeated sounds and rhythms in poetry, on meaning, tone, or mood.
6	D	Explain how an author develops the point of view of the narrator or speaker in a text.
7	A	Determine a theme or central idea of a text and how it is conveyed through particular details; provide a summary of a text distinct from personal opinions or judgments.
8	B	Determine the meaning of words and phrases as they are used in a text, including figurative and connotative meanings; analyze the impact of specific word choices, including those that create repeated sounds and rhythms in poetry, on meaning, tone, or mood.
9	See Below	Compare and contrast texts in different forms or genres in terms of their approaches to similar themes and topics.

Give a score of 0, 1, 2, 3, or 4 based on how well the answer meets the criteria listed.
- It should give a reasonable explanation of what the dog could learn from Patrick.
- The answer should relate to how the dog does not appreciate what he has, while Patrick appreciates even the little things.
- It should use relevant details from both passages.
- It should be well-organized, clear, and easy to understand.

English Language Arts, Reading Workbook, Grade 6

Set 6: Paired Informational Texts

Sugar/Sweet Tooth

Core Skills Practice

Core skill: Cite textual evidence to support analysis of what a text states explicitly as well as inferences drawn from the text, quoting or paraphrasing as appropriate.

Answer: The student should answer the questions based on the information in the passage.
- A sugar crystal is made of a fructose and a glucose molecule.
- Caramelization is the melting of the sugar crystals.

Core Skills Practice

Core skill: Determine a text's central idea(s) and how particular details help convey the idea(s); provide a summary of a text distinct from personal opinions or judgments.

Answer: The student should explain that sugarcane juice cannot be stored or transported like crystallized sugar can. Student should describe how this development caused sugar use to become more common.

Question	Answer	Reading Standard
1	D	Determine the meaning of words and phrases as they are used in a text, including figurative, connotative, and technical meanings; explain how word choice affects meaning and tone.
2	B	Determine a text's central idea(s) and how particular details help convey the idea(s); provide a summary of a text distinct from personal opinions or judgments.
3	C	Integrate information presented in different media or formats as well as in words to develop a coherent understanding of a topic or issue.
4	A	Analyze in detail how a key individual, event, or idea is introduced, illustrated, and elaborated in a text.
5	A	Determine the meaning of words and phrases as they are used in a text, including figurative, connotative, and technical meanings; explain how word choice affects meaning and tone.
6	A	Analyze how a particular sentence, paragraph, chapter, section, or text feature fits into the overall structure of a text and contributes to the development of the ideas.
7	C	Cite textual evidence to support analysis of what a text states explicitly as well as inferences drawn from the text, quoting or paraphrasing as appropriate.
8	B	Determine the meaning of words and phrases as they are used in a text, including figurative, connotative, and technical meanings; explain how word choice affects meaning and tone.
9	See Below	Analyze in detail how a key individual, event, or idea is introduced, illustrated, and elaborated in a text.

Give a score of 0, 1, 2, 3, or 4 based on how well the answer meets the criteria listed.
- It should explain how the form of sugar changes its properties and how this affects its use.
- The answer should describe how sugar caramelizes, and how this is used to make sweets.
- The answer should describe how sugar can be in the form of sugarcane juice, and how people chewed on the sugarcane to get the juice.
- The answer should describe how crystallized sugar can be stored and transported, and how this allowed sugar to be used often and to be added to foods.
- It should use relevant details from both passages.
- It should be well-organized, clear, and easy to understand.

Set 7: Literary Texts

Gone Fishing

Core Skills Practice

Core skill: Explain how an author develops the point of view of the narrator or speaker in a text.

Answer: The student should write a paragraph describing the day from Tony's point of view. The narrative should be written in first-person point of view.

Question	Answer	Reading Standard
1	A	Describe how the plot of a particular story, poem, or drama unfolds in a series of episodes as well as how the characters respond or change as the plot moves toward a resolution.
2	A	Cite textual evidence to support analysis of what a text states explicitly as well as inferences drawn from the text, quoting or paraphrasing as appropriate.
3	D	Determine a theme or central idea of a text and how it is conveyed through particular details; provide a summary of a text distinct from personal opinions or judgments.
4	C	Analyze how a particular sentence, chapter, scene, or stanza fits into the overall structure of a text and contributes to the development of the theme, setting, or plot.

The Dentist

Core Skills Practice

Core skill: Analyze how a particular sentence, chapter, scene, or stanza fits into the overall structure of a text and contributes to the development of the theme, setting, or plot.

Answer: The student should complete the table with the example and purpose below.

Letter Part	Example from the Letter	Purpose of the Part
date line	September 15, 2012	to tell when the letter was written
greeting	Dear Aunt Sienna,	to tell who the letter is to
closing	Bye for now,	to end the letter

Question	Answer	Reading Standard
1	D	Determine the meaning of words and phrases as they are used in a text, including figurative and connotative meanings; analyze the impact of specific word choices, including those that create repeated sounds and rhythms in poetry, on meaning, tone, or mood.
2	B	Describe how the plot of a particular story, poem, or drama unfolds in a series of episodes as well as how the characters respond or change as the plot moves toward a resolution.
3	B	Explain how an author develops the point of view of the narrator or speaker in a text.
4	C	Determine a theme or central idea of a text and how it is conveyed through particular details; provide a summary of a text distinct from personal opinions or judgments.

The Evil Candide

Core Skills Practice

Core skill: Compare and contrast texts in different forms or genres in terms of their approaches to similar themes and topics.

Answer: The student should identify the qualities of an epic the passage has. It should describe how it includes the prince as the hero and Candide as the villain. It may describe how the prince does a heroic deed, goes on a difficult quest, or battles against evil. It may also refer to how the passage is about good defeating evil or about a prince saving a princess.

Question	Answer	Reading Standard
1	D	Determine the meaning of words and phrases as they are used in a text, including figurative and connotative meanings; analyze the impact of specific word choices, including those that create repeated sounds and rhythms in poetry, on meaning, tone, or mood.
2	A	Analyze how a particular sentence, chapter, scene, or stanza fits into the overall structure of a text and contributes to the development of the theme, setting, or plot.
3	B	Compare and contrast texts in different forms or genres in terms of their approaches to similar themes and topics.
4	C	Determine the meaning of words and phrases as they are used in a text, including figurative and connotative meanings; analyze the impact of specific word choices, including those that create repeated sounds and rhythms in poetry, on meaning, tone, or mood.

A Quiet Night

Core Skills Practice

Core skill: Analyze the impact of specific word choices, including those that create repeated sounds and rhythms in poetry, on meaning, tone, or mood.

Answer: The student should explain that the repetition helps the reader imagine Gloria reading the book, and may also indicate that it helps create the calm mood. The student may explain the literal meaning of "drifted off" as showing that Gloria fell asleep, or may refer to how the phrase shows how relaxed and calm Gloria felt.

Question	Answer	Reading Standard
1	A	Determine the meaning of words and phrases as they are used in a text, including figurative and connotative meanings; analyze the impact of specific word choices, including those that create repeated sounds and rhythms in poetry, on meaning, tone, or mood.
2	C	Cite textual evidence to support analysis of what a text states explicitly as well as inferences drawn from the text, quoting or paraphrasing as appropriate.
3	B	Determine a theme or central idea of a text and how it is conveyed through particular details; provide a summary of a text distinct from personal opinions or judgments.
4	C	Analyze how a particular sentence, chapter, scene, or stanza fits into the overall structure of a text and contributes to the development of the theme, setting, or plot.
5	See Below	Determine the meaning of words and phrases as they are used in a text, including figurative and connotative meanings; analyze the impact of specific word choices, including those that create repeated sounds and rhythms in poetry, on meaning, tone, or mood.

Give a score of 0, 1, 2, 3, or 4 based on how well the answer meets the criteria listed.
- It should identify specific examples of words used that suggest that Gloria is relaxed.
- The words identified may include the following: *snuggled up, propped a thick pillow, turned page after page, candle slowly burned down, flickered slightly,* and *drifted off*.
- It should use relevant details from the passage.
- It should be well-organized, clear, and easy to understand.

English Language Arts, Reading Workbook, Grade 6

Set 8: Informational Texts

King of the Jungle

Core skill: Analyze in detail how a key individual, event, or idea is introduced, illustrated, and elaborated in a text.
Answer: The student may describe how lions and tigers are both members of the Felidae family, are both members of the Panthera genus, or are both one of the four big cats. The student should describe how tigers are larger than lions.

Question	Answer	Reading Standard
1	C	Determine the meaning of words and phrases as they are used in a text, including figurative, connotative, and technical meanings; explain how word choice affects meaning and tone.
2	A	Determine an author's point of view or purpose in a text and explain how it is conveyed in the text.
3	B	Trace and evaluate the argument and specific claims in a text, distinguishing claims that are supported by reasons and evidence from claims that are not.
4	D	Integrate information presented in different media or formats as well as in words to develop a coherent understanding of a topic or issue.

Be Prepared

Core Skills Practice

Core skill: Cite textual evidence to support analysis of what a text states explicitly as well as inferences drawn from the text, quoting or paraphrasing as appropriate.
Answer: The student should select one of the qualities that he or she lacks. Students should clearly explain how they would benefit from developing the selected quality.

Question	Answer	Reading Standard
1	Scouts, 11 to 18 Rover Scouts, over 18	Cite textual evidence to support analysis of what a text states explicitly as well as inferences drawn from the text, quoting or paraphrasing as appropriate.
2	C	Integrate information presented in different media or formats as well as in words to develop a coherent understanding of a topic or issue.
3	C	Determine the meaning of words and phrases as they are used in a text, including figurative, connotative, and technical meanings; explain how word choice affects meaning and tone.
4	B	Determine an author's point of view or purpose in a text and explain how it is conveyed in the text.

Black, Red, and Gold

Core Skills Practice

Core skill: Use common, grade-appropriate Greek or Latin affixes and roots as clues to the meaning of a word.

Answer: The student should list three words that contain the Latin root *tri*, and write a definition of each word. Sample answers are given below.

tripod	a stand with three legs
triangle	a shape with three sides and three angles
triathlon	a race made up of three different activities
tricycle	a cycle with three wheels
triannual	occurring three times a year / occurring every three years
trilogy	a series of three books or three films

Question	Answer	Reading Standard
1	B	Determine the meaning of words and phrases as they are used in a text, including figurative, connotative, and technical meanings; explain how word choice affects meaning and tone.
2	A	Analyze in detail how a key individual, event, or idea is introduced, illustrated, and elaborated in a text.
3	B	Analyze how a particular sentence, paragraph, chapter, section, or text feature fits into the overall structure of a text and contributes to the development of the ideas.
4	C	Determine a text's central idea(s) and how particular details help convey the idea(s); provide a summary of a text distinct from personal opinions or judgments.

Photosynthesis

Core Skills Practice

Core skill: Integrate information presented in different media or formats as well as in words to develop a coherent understanding of a topic or issue.

Answer: The student should explain why the diagram is important in the passage. The student may describe how it summarizes the process described in the passage, how it presents a complex process in a simple way, or how it helps readers visualize what is being described.

Question	Answer	Reading Standard
1	C	Determine the meaning of words and phrases as they are used in a text, including figurative, connotative, and technical meanings; explain how word choice affects meaning and tone.
2	D	Determine an author's point of view or purpose in a text and explain how it is conveyed in the text.
3	C	Cite textual evidence to support analysis of what a text states explicitly as well as inferences drawn from the text, quoting or paraphrasing as appropriate.
4	B	Analyze how a particular sentence, paragraph, chapter, section, or text feature fits into the overall structure of a text and contributes to the development of the ideas.
5	See Below	Determine a text's central idea(s) and how particular details help convey the idea(s); provide a summary of a text distinct from personal opinions or judgments.

Give a score of 0, 1, 2, 3, or 4 based on how well the answer meets the criteria listed.
- It should accurately describe the process of photosynthesis.
- It should explain that plants use photosynthesis to get energy, and describe how photosynthesis occurs.
- It should use relevant details from the passage.
- It should be well-organized, clear, and easy to understand.

English Language Arts, Reading Workbook, Grade 6

Set 9: Literary and Informational Texts

Flying Scavengers

Core Skills Practice

Core skill: Conduct short research projects to answer a question, drawing on several sources and refocusing the inquiry when appropriate.

Answer: The student should list questions that would be appropriate to answer in a report about the Andean Condor.

Question	Answer	Reading Standard
1	D	Cite textual evidence to support analysis of what a text states explicitly as well as inferences drawn from the text, quoting or paraphrasing as appropriate.
2	B	Compare and contrast one author's presentation of events with that of another.
3	D	Determine an author's point of view or purpose in a text and explain how it is conveyed in the text.
4	A	Analyze how a particular sentence, paragraph, chapter, section, or text feature fits into the overall structure of a text and contributes to the development of the ideas.

Artistic Creativity

Core Skills Practice

Core skill: Write arguments to support claims with clear reasons and relevant evidence.

Answer: The student should write a short argument about why it is important to be creative, and include the main benefits of being creative. Students may refer to the information in the passage, or may use their own ideas.

Question	Answer	Reading Standard
1	A	Determine the meaning of words and phrases as they are used in a text, including figurative, connotative, and technical meanings; explain how word choice affects meaning and tone.
2	C	Cite textual evidence to support analysis of what a text states explicitly as well as inferences drawn from the text, quoting or paraphrasing as appropriate.
3	A	Determine an author's point of view or purpose in a text and explain how it is conveyed in the text.
4	B	Determine a text's central idea(s) and how particular details help convey the idea(s); provide a summary of a text distinct from personal opinions or judgments.

English Language Arts, Reading Workbook, Grade 6

The Stanley Cup

Core Skills Practice

Core skill: Determine a text's central idea(s) and how particular details help convey the idea(s); provide a summary of a text distinct from personal opinions or judgments.

Answer: The student should use at least two details to explain why the Stanley Cup is special. Students may refer to how a new trophy is not made each year, how names are engraved on the trophy each year, or may describe the long history of the trophy.

Question	Answer	Reading Standard
1	A	Determine the meaning of words and phrases as they are used in a text, including figurative, connotative, and technical meanings; explain how word choice affects meaning and tone.
2	C	Analyze how a particular sentence, paragraph, chapter, section, or text feature fits into the overall structure of a text and contributes to the development of the ideas.
3	B	Trace and evaluate the argument and specific claims in a text, distinguishing claims that are supported by reasons and evidence from claims that are not.
4	D	Determine a text's central idea(s) and how particular details help convey the idea(s); provide a summary of a text distinct from personal opinions or judgments.

A Special Student

Core Skills Practice

Core skill: Analyze how a particular sentence, chapter, scene, or stanza fits into the overall structure of a text and contributes to the development of the theme, setting, or plot.

Answer: The student should explain why the author does not reveal that June is a cow right away and explain the effect this has on the reader. The answer may refer to how it creates interest, makes the reader wonder, adds humor, or creates an interesting surprise when it is revealed that June is a cow.

Question	Answer	Reading Standard
1	D	Explain how an author develops the point of view of the narrator or speaker in a text.
2	C	Determine a theme or central idea of a text and how it is conveyed through particular details; provide a summary of a text distinct from personal opinions or judgments.
3	D	Describe how the plot of a particular story, poem, or drama unfolds in a series of episodes as well as how the characters respond or change as the plot moves toward a resolution.
4	A	Determine the meaning of words and phrases as they are used in a text, including figurative and connotative meanings; analyze the impact of specific word choices, including those that create repeated sounds and rhythms in poetry, on meaning, tone, or mood.
5	See Below	Cite textual evidence to support analysis of what a text states explicitly as well as inferences drawn from the text, quoting or paraphrasing as appropriate.

Give a score of 0, 1, 2, 3, or 4 based on how well the answer meets the criteria listed.
- It should provide a fully-supported explanation of how you can tell that June receives excellent care.
- It may refer to how she enjoys having students milk her, is allowed out to graze, has shelter, or is always being patted by students.
- It should use relevant details from the passage.
- It should be well-organized, clear, and easy to understand.

English Language Arts, Reading Workbook, Grade 6

Set 10: Literary and Informational Texts

Cartoons

Core Skills Practice

Core skill: Write arguments to support claims with clear reasons and relevant evidence.
Answer: The student should give an opinion on whether they think cartoons are silly or entertaining, and should support the opinion with a valid explanation. The response can refer to the passage, but should be based mainly on the student's own ideas.

Question	Answer	Reading Standard
1	B	Determine the meaning of words and phrases as they are used in a text, including figurative and connotative meanings; analyze the impact of specific word choices, including those that create repeated sounds and rhythms in poetry, on meaning, tone, or mood.
2	D	Determine a theme or central idea of a text and how it is conveyed through particular details; provide a summary of a text distinct from personal opinions or judgments.
3	A	Analyze how a particular sentence, chapter, scene, or stanza fits into the overall structure of a text and contributes to the development of the theme, setting, or plot.
4	A	Explain how an author develops the point of view of the narrator or speaker in a text.

Troy McClure

Core Skills Practice

Core skill: Determine an author's point of view or purpose in a text and explain how it is conveyed in the text.
Answer: The student should make an inference about how the author feels about the retirement of Troy McClure. The inference should be that the author feels sadness or disappointment about the retirement. The student should clearly explain how you can tell that the author feels this way.

Question	Answer	Reading Standard
1	A	Determine the meaning of words and phrases as they are used in a text, including figurative, connotative, and technical meanings; explain how word choice affects meaning and tone.
2	C	Cite textual evidence to support analysis of what a text states explicitly as well as inferences drawn from the text, quoting or paraphrasing as appropriate.
3	B	Integrate information presented in different media or formats as well as in words to develop a coherent understanding of a topic or issue.
4	A	Determine the meaning of words and phrases as they are used in a text, including figurative, connotative, and technical meanings; explain how word choice affects meaning and tone.

English Language Arts, Reading Workbook, Grade 6

The Park

Core Skills Practice

Core skill: Cite textual evidence to support analysis of what a text states explicitly as well as inferences drawn from the text, quoting or paraphrasing as appropriate.

Answer: The student should infer that the man was pretending to be a statue to make money and to entertain, or may refer to the man as a busker or street artist.

Question	Answer	Reading Standard
1	A	Determine the meaning of words and phrases as they are used in a text, including figurative and connotative meanings; analyze the impact of specific word choices, including those that create repeated sounds and rhythms in poetry, on meaning, tone, or mood.
2	Having picnics, rowing boats, feeding ducks, lazing around, or reading	Determine a theme or central idea of a text and how it is conveyed through particular details; provide a summary of a text distinct from personal opinions or judgments.
3	C	Analyze how a particular sentence, chapter, scene, or stanza fits into the overall structure of a text and contributes to the development of the theme, setting, or plot.
4	C	Compare and contrast the experience of reading a story, drama, or poem to that of listening to or viewing the same text.

Breaking In

Core Skills Practice

Core skill: Determine a text's central idea(s) and how particular details help convey the idea(s); provide a summary of a text distinct from personal opinions or judgments.

Answer: The student should describe how the passage has a lesson about taking a chance and being different. The student should refer to how the iMac G3 was very different at the time and how this made it a great success.

Question	Answer	Reading Standard
1	B	Determine the meaning of words and phrases as they are used in a text, including figurative, connotative, and technical meanings; explain how word choice affects meaning and tone.
2	B	Determine an author's point of view or purpose in a text and explain how it is conveyed in the text.
3	B	Trace and evaluate the argument and specific claims in a text, distinguishing claims that are supported by reasons and evidence from claims that are not.
4	A	Determine the meaning of words and phrases as they are used in a text, including figurative, connotative, and technical meanings; explain how word choice affects meaning and tone.
5	See Below	Determine a text's central idea(s) and how particular details help convey the idea(s); provide a summary of a text distinct from personal opinions or judgments.

Give a score of 0, 1, 2, 3, or 4 based on how well the answer meets the criteria listed.
- It should explain why the iMac G3 was very successful.
- It may refer to how it was different from most computers at the time, how it took up less space because of its unique design with the computer parts in the monitor, how people liked the design, or how people liked its bright colors and the way it looked.
- It should use relevant details from the passage.
- It should be well-organized, clear, and easy to understand.

English Language Arts, Reading Workbook, Grade 6

Set 11: Paired Literary Texts

The Astronomer/Drummer Boy

Core Skills Practice
Core skill: Describe how the plot of a particular story, poem, or drama unfolds in a series of episodes as well as how the characters respond or change as the plot moves toward a resolution.
Answer: The student should infer that the astronomer is annoyed or frustrated about being stuck in the well. Students may refer to the astronomer's actions, such as how he groaned and pummeled his fists against the well. The student may also refer to how the astronomer feels like the stars are laughing at him.

Core Skills Practice
Core skill: Analyze how a particular sentence, chapter, scene, or stanza fits into the overall structure of a text and contributes to the development of the theme, setting, or plot.
Answer: The student should describe how you can tell that Tim gets lost in his daydream. The answer could refer to how he doesn't notice students glaring at him, how he gets louder and louder, or how he imagines that the quiet classroom is the silent crowd.

Question	Answer	Reading Standard
1	A	Determine the meaning of words and phrases as they are used in a text, including figurative and connotative meanings; analyze the impact of specific word choices, including those that create repeated sounds and rhythms in poetry, on meaning, tone, or mood.
2	B	Compare and contrast texts in different forms or genres in terms of their approaches to similar themes and topics.
3	D	Determine a theme or central idea of a text and how it is conveyed through particular details; provide a summary of a text distinct from personal opinions or judgments.
4	D	Analyze how a particular sentence, chapter, scene, or stanza fits into the overall structure of a text and contributes to the development of the theme, setting, or plot.
5	C	Determine the meaning of words and phrases as they are used in a text, including figurative and connotative meanings; analyze the impact of specific word choices, including those that create repeated sounds and rhythms in poetry, on meaning, tone, or mood.
6	A	Determine a theme or central idea of a text and how it is conveyed through particular details; provide a summary of a text distinct from personal opinions or judgments.
7	D	Analyze how a particular sentence, chapter, scene, or stanza fits into the overall structure of a text and contributes to the development of the theme, setting, or plot.
8	C	Explain how an author develops the point of view of the narrator or speaker in a text.
9	See Below	Compare and contrast texts in different forms or genres in terms of their approaches to similar themes and topics.

Give a score of 0, 1, 2, 3, or 4 based on how well the answer meets the criteria listed.
- It should describe how the astronomer and Tim learn similar lessons.
- The answer may refer to them both learning to pay attention to where they are, not getting lost in their own thoughts, or concentrating on what they should be doing and not the hobby or interest they have.
- It should use relevant details from both passages.
- It should be well-organized, clear, and easy to understand.

English Language Arts, Reading Workbook, Grade 6

Set 12: Paired Informational Texts

Radiohead/Like a Rolling Stone

Core Skills Practice
Core skill: Cite textual evidence to support analysis of what a text states explicitly as well as inferences drawn from the text, quoting or paraphrasing as appropriate.
Answer: The student should give an opinion on whether or not it is worthwhile for bands to keep trying despite the low likelihood of achieving success, and should support the opinion with a valid explanation. The answer could argue that Radiohead were lucky to achieve success or could argue that the chance they took was worth it because they did so well in the end.

Core Skills Practice
Core skill: Determine an author's point of view or purpose in a text and explain how it is conveyed in the text.
Answer: The student should give a reasonable explanation of how the author seems to feel. The answer may describe how the author seems to like, admire, or respect the band. The student may refer to specific phrases used like "stood the test of time," specific words used like "amazingly," the tone of the passage, or how all the information given is positive and praises the band.

Question	Answer	Reading Standard
1	B	Trace and evaluate the argument and specific claims in a text, distinguishing claims that are supported by reasons and evidence from claims that are not.
2	B	Analyze how a particular sentence, paragraph, chapter, section, or text feature fits into the overall structure of a text and contributes to the development of the ideas.
3	A	Determine an author's point of view or purpose in a text and explain how it is conveyed in the text.
4	D	Determine the meaning of words and phrases as they are used in a text, including figurative, connotative, and technical meanings; explain how word choice affects meaning and tone.
5	B	Determine the meaning of words and phrases as they are used in a text, including figurative, connotative, and technical meanings; explain how word choice affects meaning and tone.
6	C	Trace and evaluate the argument and specific claims in a text, distinguishing claims that are supported by reasons and evidence from claims that are not.
7	C	Determine an author's point of view or purpose in a text and explain how it is conveyed in the text.
8	D	Analyze in detail how a key individual, event, or idea is introduced, illustrated, and elaborated in a text.
9	See Below	Compare and contrast one author's presentation of events with that of another.
10	See Below	Compare and contrast one author's presentation of events with that of another.

Q9.
Give a score of 0, 1, or 2 based on how well the answer meets the criteria listed.
- It should give a reasonable comparison of how information is presented in the two passages.
- It may describe how both passages describe the history of a band, how both passages present details about the success of a band, or how both passages include facts about a band's achievements.

Q10.
Give a score of 0, 1, or 2 based on how well the answer meets the criteria listed.
- It should explain how you can tell that The Rolling Stones are more successful than Radiohead.
- It may refer to how The Rolling Stones have lasted since 1962 versus 1985, have released 30 albums versus eight, and have sold 200 million albums versus 25 million.

Made in the USA
Middletown, DE
19 March 2018